America, You Have Some Explaining to Do

Darnell L. King-Cason

Published by Darnell L. King-Cason, 2024.

In the King James Version (KJV) of the Bible, the command to love yourself in relation to loving your neighbor can be found in Matthew 22:39. It states:

"And the second is like unto it, Thou shalt love thy neighbour as thyself."

This verse emphasizes the importance of loving others in the same way that you love yourself, highlighting the connection between self-love and love for others.

Preface

In a world where the complexities of race, history, and personal identity intersect, I have embarked on a journey to share my reflections, experiences, and lessons learned throughout my life. This book is not just a collection of stories; it is a heartfelt exploration of love, resilience, and the unbreakable spirit of the African American community.

As I reflect on my life as a husband, father, and son, I am reminded of the importance of understanding our past to shape a better future. The struggles faced by my ancestors echo in the stories of those who came before me, from the horrors of slavery to the triumphs of self-made communities like Black Wall Street. Through these pages, I aim to pay homage to their sacrifices while encouraging future generations to embrace their heritage with pride and strength.

This book also addresses the uncomfortable truths of racism, the impact of systemic oppression, and the nuances of human relationships. It serves as a reminder that not every individual is defined by their race or experiences, urging compassion and understanding in a world too often divided by color.

I share my reflections not only to recount my personal journey but also to ignite conversations that can lead to healing and unity. The path to understanding one another begins with dialogue, and it is my hope that this book will inspire readers to engage in that essential conversation.

Join me as we navigate the complexities of our shared humanity, recognizing that while our stories may differ, our struggles and dreams are deeply intertwined. Together, let us strive for a future filled with love, respect, and understanding.

Disclaimer

"The content in this book discusses well-documented historical events and situations that are part of the public domain. This includes information about the experiences of Black individuals and communities throughout American history, covering instances of racial violence, systemic oppression, and significant cultural contributions. All references to these events are based on widely accepted historical accounts and publicly available sources. Therefore, the information can be freely discussed and published without fear of copyright infringement or legal action for defamation. This book aims to educate, inform, and encourage dialogue about these important issues while honoring the legacy and experiences of those affected by these historical injustices." These historical injustices.

Thank You

I want to express my gratitude to my family for allowing me the time to focus on creating this book. I know I've been a bit of a wreck lately, consumed by my writing, but I truly appreciate your support. To my wife and children, you are the best. I love you always.

My Mother, Ruth N King. My Father, Joseph Cason. Mother-in-law Cordene Sinkler. Aunt Maureen Sinkler. Demetrius Sinkler. Kevin Wilson. Shakira Sinkler. Uncle Samuel Sinkler. Grandpa Cyde Sinkler(R.I.P) Father inlaw, Michael Jones. (rip)- Hakim Sinkler (rip)Lamont Cason Brother-in-law, Damon Jones. Taurean Brown Brother, Don Adams. Cousin, Garrett Wilson. Cousin, Christian Wilson. Aunt Linda D Parker. Naquan Collins. Daniel Scudder and Becky Scudder. Bernard Bradshaw.Phil Phil. Makel Ali. David Massey. Aunt Neat. Cousin, Phoenix Badmus.Cousin. Dee frazier(rip) Sister, Latanya Harrell. Sister, Tawanda Cason. Sister, Yvonne M.NewsdomeBracys Sister Sherell Myers. Cousin, Yvette Frazier. Nancy Gonzalez. Paul Stewart. Andria Norton.

Chris Simmons. khalif Jones. Vesso/Vick. 100proof/Elliott.Don Hernandez. Dominique Hughes. Chiquita Hughes, Stephine Hughes, Grandma, Vivian & Grandpa Benny. William Jenkins. Tymika Jackson.

MH Foryth Heinemann. Jamar Gregory. Edwardo Donato. (rip)Lisa Moore. Gerald Hill Jermine M. King Cason Nicole King-Cason

Donna Thompson. Joe Massai. Dawn Claire. Tony Davis.

Faith Herb. Zack Caz Mackey. Rosemary Kaleo.

Antonio Gray. Jermaine Brown Jay Eldemire

Dedication

This chapter is dedicated to the valiant individuals who have fought for civil rights and to those who have endured suffering due to racial injustice.

To Martin Luther King Jr., whose vision of equality continues to guide us;

To Rosa Parks, whose quiet courage ignited a movement for change;

To John Lewis, whose commitment to justice taught us the power of standing up for what is right;

To Malcolm X, who spoke boldly for the rights of Black Americans;

To Medgar Evers, whose dedication to civil rights cost him his life;

To Coretta Scott King, who carried forward the legacy of her husband with strength and determination;

To Emmett Till, whose tragic story serves as a reminder of the need for justice.

To the resilient survivors of Black Wall Street: Olivia J. Hooker, Viola Fletcher, Hughes Van Ellis, and Lessie Benningfield Randle—your endurance in the face of adversity inspires us all.

And to every individual who has faced harm and injustice simply because of their Black identity—your experiences are woven into the fabric of our struggle for equality. May your stories motivate future generations to continue the fight for justice and change.

Prologue

For years, the debate over granting reparations to the descendants of slaves in America has persisted. Some contend that it would be unjust for the majority to compensate the minority, particularly African Americans, whose forebears were sold into slavery by Europeans. For over 400 years, African slaves suffered immensely – enduring mutilation, rape, murder, and extreme labor without remuneration. Most labored in cotton fields until their hands bled, with any dissent met with ruthless punishment, including severe beatings.

Their living conditions were appalling, with many confined to shacks barely larger than chicken coops. They were regarded as subhuman, with even animals receiving better treatment. The terror of their lives, thrust into an alien land, stripped of their language, culture, and dignity, is unfathomable. The thought of enduring such relentless mistreatment and degradation is devastating.

The legacy of slavery continues, as many African Americans find it difficult to trace their ancestry due to slavery's disruption. Although a few have succeeded in tracing their roots, such cases are exceptional. Moreover, it's critical to recognize that most black Americans descend from those who were involuntarily brought here as slaves, despite the fact that some Africans migrated to the United States by choice.

The claim that Africans sold other Africans into slavery is frequently used to shift blame, yet it overlooks the significant role Europeans played in sustaining the slave trade. Furthermore, the trade of humans is a crime against humanity, irrespective of the perpetrators involved.

America's history is marred by racism and oppression, and failing to confront and rectify this past only continues the cycle of injustice. Reparations represent more than just monetary recompense.

TO THE FAMILY AND COMMUNITY

As I reflect on the stories and events discussed in this book, I cannot help but think of my own family and the relatives who have suffered from the injustices that have plagued Black communities throughout history. If any of you have experienced the pain of racial violence, systemic oppression, or the loss of a loved one due to these unfortunate circumstances, my heart aches for you. You are in my prayers, and I want you to know that you are not alone in your sorrow.

It is deeply saddening that anyone should endure such suffering. The experiences shared in this book are not merely historical accounts; they are the echoes of pain that still resonate today. They remind us of the resilience of our ancestors and the challenges that many in our communities continue to face.

This book is dedicated to you, to honor the memories of those who are no longer here and to shine a light on the struggles that have shaped our lives. May it serve as a testament to the strength and love that persist despite the hardships we have faced. I hope it can provide some solace to those left behind, reminding you that the stories of our loved ones will never be forgotten and that their legacy lives on in our hearts.

As we navigate the complexities of our shared history, let us strive to learn from the past and work towards a future where such injustices are no longer tolerated. Together, we can honor the memories of our loved ones and ensure that their stories are told, acknowledged, and celebrated.

Introduction: The Legacy contradiction

America was founded on the promise of liberty, justice, and equality for all, ideals enshrined in the Constitution and celebrated on national holidays. However, the reality of America's history reveals a different story, one of deep contradictions and persistent inequalities. At the heart of this system is the legacy of racism, a legacy that has been interwoven into the nation's fabric from the start.

Is racism in America simply a thing of the past, or is it an active force that continues to shape our society? It's evident that it remains a present-day issue. If not addressed, it may well continue to affect our future. From the arrival of the first enslaved Africans in the 1500s, racial oppression has been intrinsically linked with the United States' economic, social, and political development. The early wealth and power of America were largely built on the labor of enslaved Black people, whose forced labor propelled the American economy.

Did the abolition of slavery mark the end of racism, or did it herald a new era of racial oppression, characterized by the harsh enforcement of Jim Crow laws, the systematic disenfranchisement of Black citizens, and the institutionalization of segregation? For almost a century post-Civil War, Black Americans were denied their fundamental rights, subjected to violence and intimidation, and relegated to second-class citizenship in a country that professed to uphold freedom and equality.

The Civil Rights Movement of the 1950s and 1960s led to significant changes, with landmark legislation such as the Civil Rights Act of 1964 and the Voting Rights Act of 1965 breaking down legal barriers of segregation and opening new opportunities for Black Americans. However, the movement did not erase the entrenched racism that still affects our society. Structural inequalities in education, housing, employment, and criminal justice remain, perpetuating poverty and disenfranchisement that disproportionately impact people of color.

Today, the legacy of racism in America is still evident. The deaths of unarmed Black individuals by police, the persistent racial wealth gap, and the health disparities exposed by the COVID-19 pandemic show that racial injustice is not a relic of the past. These issues are not isolated but are the result of centuries of systemic racism, a deeply embedded system of oppression that has influenced every aspect of American life.

Confronting this legacy involves acknowledging uncomfortable truths about its maintenance and perpetuation. Racism in America has been institutionalized through laws, policies, and practices that systematically disadvantage Black people and other people of color, reinforced by cultural narratives that dehumanize those who are different, and upheld by a social and economic order that privileges some at the expense of others.

Addressing these truths is a start, but to truly reckon with this legacy, steps must be taken to dismantle the structures of racism that continue to oppress and marginalize people of color. Each person, as an individual and as a member of society, has a role in creating a more just and equitable America.

The History African woman

One of the most damaging legacies of this stereotype is its impact on healthcare. Even today, Black women are often not taken seriously when they express pain or discomfort in medical settings. Studies have shown that they are less likely to receive adequate pain management compared to their white counterparts, a direct result of the lingering belief that they can endure more pain. This has led to tragic outcomes, with Black women facing higher rates of maternal mortality and complications during childbirth.

The perception of invincibility carries a significant emotional and psychological toll. Black women are frequently seen as the pillars of their families and communities, shouldering everyone's burdens while neglecting their own. The constant demand to remain resilient limits their chance to express vulnerability, perpetuating a cycle in which their own struggles are overlooked by others and downplayed by themselves.

Despite facing numerous challenges, Black women have consistently shown remarkable resilience and strength. They have played a pivotal role in social justice movements, advocating not just for their rights, but for the rights of all oppressed individuals. They have provided care for their families, guided their communities, and fostered environments of love and support that facilitate healing and mutual empowerment.

However, this strength should not be mistaken for an infinite capacity to endure suffering. It is crucial to recognize that Black women, like all human beings, experience pain, fear, and vulnerability. They deserve to be seen, heard, and treated with the dignity and compassion that has so often been denied to them.

As we reflect on the history of how Black women have been treated, it is imperative to challenge the stereotypes that have justified their mistreatment. We must listen to their voices, acknowledge their pain, and work to dismantle the systems that continue to oppress them. Only then can we begin to honor the full humanity of Black women, recognizing not only their strength but also their right to be cared for, respected, and cherished.

Common Misconception of Enslaved Africans and the Bible

There's a common misconception about Africans being introduced to Christianity by Europeans, but this is not accurate. In fact, evidence shows that Africans were Christians long before American influence. Christianity in Africa dates back to ancient times, especially in regions like Ethiopia, where one of the earliest Christian kingdoms was established. The reason Europeans and later Americans are often credited with introducing Christianity to Africans is largely due to language differences. When European missionaries encountered Africans, they didn't recognize the existing Christian traditions because they were practiced in languages like Swahili and other tribal dialects, not in English.

For instance, Swahili Bibles existed, and Christianity was practiced in parts of Africa long before European colonization. This area of Africa, often referred to as the cradle of civilization, is also where our Lord and Savior, Jesus Christ, walked on Earth. The Bible was introduced to African slaves by their oppressors, but this was not the introduction of Christianity itself—only the English language. Africans already knew about the Bible in their languages.

Imagine an experiment where you place five people who speak different languages in a room and talk to them about the Bible in English. If they don't respond, it might seem like they don't understand Christianity. But if you had an interpreter, you'd find that they do know the Bible, just in their own languages. So, the notion that Europeans were the first to introduce Christianity to Africans is like saying Christopher Columbus discovered America—a narrative that overlooks the presence of people who were already there.

The only thing the oppressors truly taught the Africans was their language, not the Bible itself, which the Africans already knew in their own tongues. We often give too much credit to those from the past who don't deserve it. Even a lie, if repeated often enough, can begin to sound like the truth—even to the one who invented it.

When we think about the origins of Christianity, our minds often drift to Europe—the cathedrals, the Vatican, and the long history of the Church there. But the truth is, Christianity's roots in Africa run deep, much deeper than many realize. Ethiopia, in particular, stands as a testament to the early and profound presence of Christianity on the African continent.

Long before European nations embraced Christianity, Ethiopia had already established one of the world's oldest Christian churches, the Ethiopian Orthodox Tewahedo Church. This wasn't just a small, isolated community; it was a vibrant and fully recognized state religion by the 4th century CE. King Ezana of the Aksumite Empire, whose conversion around 330 CE marked a significant moment in history, made Christianity the official religion of his kingdom. This happened even before the Roman Empire formally adopted Christianity.

What this means is that Ethiopia had a thriving Christian culture while much of Europe was still grappling with pagan beliefs or in the early stages of Christian conversion. The Ethiopian Church developed on its own, independent of the European churches, which allowed it to preserve many ancient practices and texts that have since faded or changed in other parts of the Christian world. The liturgy, still performed in the ancient Ge'ez language, and the unique canon of scriptures used by the Ethiopian Orthodox Church, are powerful symbols of a rich and unbroken Christian tradition that has endured for centuries.

This early Christian presence in Ethiopia opens up a fascinating perspective on the spiritual lives of Africans before the onset of European colonization and the horrors of the transatlantic slave trade. It's entirely possible, and indeed likely, that some Africans knew about Jesus Christ long before they were forcibly taken from their homeland. The story of the Kingdom of Kongo is a case in point. When

Portuguese explorers and missionaries arrived in West Africa, they encountered a kingdom that was receptive to the Christian faith. King Nzinga a Nkuwu and his son, King Afonso I, embraced Christianity and worked to spread its teachings among their people.

So, when we consider the Africans who were later enslaved and brought to the Americas, it's important to remember that some of them might have already been Christians. They would have had knowledge of the Bible, either through translations or through the teachings passed down by missionaries. Their faith was not something imposed upon them after they arrived in a foreign land; it was something they carried with them across the ocean, a part of their identity that persisted despite the dehumanizing conditions of slavery.

This chapter is a reflection on the rich Christian heritage that existed in Africa long before the first slave ships set sail. It challenges the often simplistic narrative that Christianity was a European import to Africa, and instead, it honors the deep, ancient roots of the faith on the continent. It's a reminder that the story of Christianity in Africa is not one of mere conversion, but of a longstanding and enduring faith that has shaped the lives of countless people over the centuries.

We are Americans right?

In my view, it's ironic that the emphasis is on aiding Americans who require financial help and housing to survive, yet no one discusses the funds our political leaders allocate to foreign nations. These American dollars are distributed globally as though they were limitless. The welfare system, aimed at the welfare of not only African Americans but all citizens, should not be contentious. The true issue lies in the expenditure and distribution of money that does not benefit any American. If we cease viewing our next-door neighbors as adversaries and instead concentrate on mutual upliftment, transcending nationalities and diverse life experiences, we could become exemplary Americans.

Yet, the persistent divide-and-conquer strategy, passed down through generations, has created a domino effect, akin to crabs in a barrel where no one wishes to see another succeed. Even those who perceive themselves as superior fail to recognize their descent. The wealthy maintain their status by fostering division, utilizing race to pit one group against another, convincing one faction of their superiority. Behind the scenes, the affluent smirk as the political stratagem endures through ages.

It's time to set the record straight, but I must warn you—the truth hurts. I truly doubt that once things are revealed about how society has been manipulated into falling into the plan that was set many years ago, it will open up some eyes. African Americans won't be the only ones awakened anymore. America has been in debt from the beginning of time, or at least it's believed to be, but that's a whole other book.

If we learned as Americans to appreciate each other and understand the differences and why things are the way they are, we could make a major change in society. If we applied what we learned and taught it to our offspring, not only could we make a better place, but we could actually pass it down to our children's children, making it a better world for those to come.

Whenever you look at something from the perspective of selfishness and don't try to look out for your neighbor, it comes back to haunt you. It's like seeing someone break into your neighbor's home, but because you don't like how they look or how they talk, you decide not to call the cops. You couldn't care less what happens, instead of thinking, "That's my neighbor; let me help him by calling the cops to make sure everything's OK." You let prejudice and ignorance take over, and you fail to understand that once the burglar is done stealing from that house and there's nothing else to take, your home is next.

You could've eliminated the problem before it started by helping your neighbor. That's why I am a true believer in what God says about loving thy neighbor as thyself. If you love your neighbor as yourself, whatever positive actions you take to help them will ripple down to you and eventually help you out in the long run. That's how America should be.

Yes, we are all different, and yes, there are some things that need to change inside the African American community, but that doesn't excuse the possibilities of what could happen positively with the right support, including financial support, to build a better America with reparations.

The Word NIGGER!

The word "nigger" is a derogatory statement toward African Americans. It was used by the oppressor to strip away their self-esteem, dignity, respect, and even a bit of their humanity.

It deeply saddens me to still hear the word "nigger" because it reflects a painful, and dehumanizing experience for African Americans, who were subjected to racism, slavery, and systematic oppression.

The African slave had already been dehumanized by their oppressors—stripped of their freedoms and subjected to enslavement, being called property as if they were mere items.

It is very important to understand what is being said here: we are talking about a person, not a thing—a human being. The brutal institution of slavery saw Black men, women, and children of all ages being sold like commodities, auctioned off, and treated as less than human. This was inhumane treatment they endured—a generation of Black people with a history of painful agony, struggles, and a search for equality.

I hate reflecting on the dark chapters of this history, although I must remind you of the importance of understanding what happened and never forgetting it. The victims of this inhumane tragedy need to be remembered for their suffering. We must not forget so that the past will never be repeated, and we should strive our best to create the best future with respect, values, and empathy for others, no matter what nationality a person is. No one should be a slave.

African Americans were treated like property, implying that they were merely objects to be owned by others, with no rights, no dignity, and no respect. Even though African American history is often neglected, it is crucial to acknowledge the impact of the African American experience and how it went against humanity the sad part about this is that African Americans were looked at as non-human beings by those in power. They were treated poorly under the brutal institution of slavery.

Black men, women, and children were sold like commodities, treated like property the way you would sell a house, a car, or even worse, like you would sell a dog. Europeans at the time did not see Africans as anything better than property—no more, no less. The pain of slavery left an impact on generations of African Americans, shaping their future and determining their struggles in America.

Despite the hardships, African Americans tried to keep their dignity and America today is still, unfortunately, experiencing racism. The heavy burden of the past continues to carry into the present. Communities in African American cities have physically and mentally collapsed due to systematic racism, prejudice, and discrimination. The scars are still there, regardless of how much some may wish they were healed so that everyone could just live their lives as if it never happened.

We African Americans have always been clever in being unique when it comes to taking something meant to be negative towards us and turning it into a positive for our benefit. The word "Nigger" has always been a negative term used against Black people. Though another word, "Nigga," is often used in urban neighborhoods, it's not necessarily better. The difference lies in that "Nigga" was created by African Americans and is used among African Americans and other people of African descent.

Many people question why this word is even used, considering the origins of how it came about. This concern is understandable. I'm not advocating for its use, but I am saying that we have been known to take what has been used against us and turn it into something that works for us. The same thing happened with food. When we were given leftovers and made fun of for eating scraps, we turned them into what is now known as Soul food. Again, I'm not claiming the food is necessarily good for our health. But like the word "Nigga," it became a part of our culture. It's a saying among popular people who call each other by that word to the point where everyone now wants to be popular and either be called that or say it, but nobody wants to be a "Nigger."

I remember being on a bus and hearing two Caucasian boys in the back, cursing at each other during a fight. As I was about to break it up, one of them said the most shocking thing that I didn't expect to hear. He called the other boy a "Nigga." I was flabbergasted.

The Emancipation Proclamation (A start towards the Ending)

Abraham Lincoln's early political career did not present him as a staunch abolitionist. In fact, his views on slavery were shaped by a pragmatic approach to the Union rather than a moral stance against the institution itself. Initially, Lincoln's priority was preserving the Union, even if it meant tolerating slavery where it already existed. However, as the Civil War unfolded, his views began to shift, influenced by the demands of war and the growing moral imperative to end slavery. The backdrop of the Emancipation Proclamation was a nation torn apart by civil war. The conflict, which began in March 4, 1861: Abraham Lincoln is inaugurated as the 16th President of the United States. At this time, he publicly states that he has no intention of abolishing slavery where it exists, but he opposes its expansion., was fueled by deep-seated issues the midst of the American Civil War, President Abraham Lincoln issued the Emancipation Proclamation on January 1, 1863. This pivotal executive order declared the freedom of all enslaved individuals in the Confederate states that were in rebellion against the Union. While the proclamation did not immediately free all enslaved people, it marked a crucial turning point in the fight against slavery in the United States.

all surrounding slavery and states' rights. As the war progressed, Lincoln recognized that the abolition of slavery was not only a moral imperative but also a strategic necessity to weaken the Confederacy and bolster the Union's war effort.

History has a way of highlighting certain moments that shape the course of a nation. Abraham Lincoln's presidency is one such moment, marked by his pivotal role in the abolition of slavery—a cause that culminated in the American Civil War. The complexity of Lincoln's journey towards emancipation, coupled with his untimely assassination, leaves us with lingering questions: Was his death a mere coincidence, or was there a plot to eliminate him before he could fully realize the liberation of African Americans.

The Emancipation Proclamation, issued on January 1, 1863, was a turning point in Lincoln's presidency. This executive order declared that all slaves in Confederate-held territory were to be set free. Although it did not immediately free all slaves, it fundamentally altered the character of the war, turning it into a fight not just for the Union, but also for human freedom. Lincoln's decision to issue the proclamation was met with both support and opposition, reflecting the deep divisions within the country.

November 19, 1863: Lincoln delivers the Gettysburg Address, where he speaks of a "new birth of freedom" and the necessity of ensuring that "government of the people, by the people, for the people, shall not perish from the earth." This speech further solidifies the Union's commitment to ending slavery.

April 9, 1865: The Civil War effectively ends with General Robert E. Lee's surrender at Appomattox Court House. The Union is preserved, and the path is set for the abolition of slavery.

April 14, 1865: Just days after the war's end, Abraham Lincoln is assassinated by John Wilkes Booth while attending a play at Ford's Theatre in Washington, D.C. Lincoln succumbs to his injuries the following day, on April 15, 1865.

The Assassination: Coincidence or Conspiracy?

The assassination of Abraham Lincoln has been the subject of much speculation and debate. John Wilkes Booth, a Confederate sympathizer, claimed responsibility for the act, but many have wondered whether there was a broader conspiracy at play. Booth's motives were clear—he believed that by killing Lincoln, he could revive the Confederate cause and prevent the complete abolition of slavery.

Some historians have pondered whether there were others who had a vested interest in Lincoln's death. Was it a calculated move to stop Lincoln from fully implementing his plans for Reconstruction and the integration of freed slaves into American society? Or was it merely the tragic act of a lone gunman driven by fanaticism?

Lincoln's Changing Views on African Americans

One of the most fascinating aspects of Lincoln's presidency is his evolving view of African Americans. Early in his career, Lincoln's opposition to slavery was largely political; he believed that the institution was morally wrong, but he was not initially an advocate for full equality between races. However, as the war progressed and he interacted with abolitionists like Frederick Douglass, Lincoln's views began to change.

By the time he issued the Emancipation Proclamation, Lincoln had come to see African Americans not just as a political issue, but as individuals deserving of freedom and dignity. His willingness to allow African Americans to serve in the Union Army was a significant step towards recognizing their humanity and contribution to the nation.

The Legacy of Abraham Lincoln

Abraham Lincoln's legacy is one of complexity and contradiction. He is hailed as the Great Emancipator, yet his journey towards embracing the full humanity of African Americans was gradual and fraught with challenges. His assassination cut short the possibility of seeing how he would have navigated the Reconstruction era and the integration of freed slaves into American society.

Was Lincoln's death a result of a broader conspiracy to prevent the full realization of his vision for a free and united America? Or was it simply the act of a disgruntled individual? These questions continue to haunt history, leaving us to ponder what might have been if Lincoln had lived.

As we reflect on the life and death of Abraham Lincoln, we must thank him for the courage to change his views and the determination to pursue emancipation. Without his leadership, the world as we know it today might be very different. Rest in peace, Abraham Lincoln, a man whose vision helped shape the course of history

The proclamation explicitly stated that "all persons held as slaves" within the rebellious states "are, and henceforward shall be free." However, it is important to note that the order applied only to the states in rebellion and did not affect enslaved individuals in border states loyal to the Union or in areas already under Union control. This limitation meant that while it was a significant step toward freedom for many, enforcement varied widely, and many enslaved people remained in bondage for years after its issuance.

Lincoln's decision to issue the Emancipation Proclamation was also influenced by the changing attitudes of the public and the abolitionist movement. The growing abolitionist sentiment in the North and the tireless efforts of activists highlighted the urgent need for change. Furthermore, as the war continued, enslaved individuals began to escape to Union lines, seeking refuge and freedom, which further demonstrated the unsustainable nature of the institution of slavery.

The proclamation had profound implications beyond its immediate effects. It transformed the Civil War from a battle for the Union into a struggle for freedom, making the fight against slavery a central goal of the conflict. This shift in focus galvanized support for the Union cause and encouraged many formerly enslaved people to join the Union Army, contributing significantly to the war effort.

Despite the limitations of the Emancipation Proclamation, it laid the groundwork for the eventual passage of the Thirteenth Amendment in 1865, which formally abolished slavery throughout the United States. The proclamation symbolized a commitment to the principles of liberty and equality, inspiring generations to continue the fight for civil rights and justice.

In reflecting on the Emancipation Proclamation, we recognize its historical significance as a bold declaration of freedom and a catalyst for change. It serves as a reminder of the struggles endured by countless individuals in the quest for liberty and the enduring legacy of their fight for justice in America. The proclamation not only altered the course of the Civil War but also set in motion a broader movement toward equality that would echo throughout American history.

The Red Summer of 1919

In 1919, known as the "Red Summer," the United States saw a surge in racial violence. After World War I, the country faced social unrest, economic instability, and heightened racial tensions. African American soldiers, who had bravely fought for their country, returned home only to face continued racial prejudices. Instead of receiving the respect and equality they had hoped for, many experienced hostility and resentment, leading to a series of violent confrontations throughout the summer.

The Red Summer witnessed over three dozen race riots across the country, with notable incidents in major cities like Chicago, Washington D.C., and Elaine, Arkansas. Factors such as job competition, housing shortages, and the fear of the growing assertiveness of African Americans fueled the violence.

One significant event took place in Chicago on July 27, 1919, when a young Black teenager named Eugene Williams accidentally crossed a racial boundary at a segregated beach, leading to his death. This sparked a deadly riot, resulting in 38 deaths—23 Black and 15 white—and over 500 injuries. The destruction was immense, with thousands of Black families losing their homes as white mobs set fire to houses in predominantly Black neighborhoods.

Similar violence occurred in Washington D.C., where racial tensions erupted, leading to deadly clashes. In Elaine, Arkansas, a meeting of Black sharecroppers demanding fair treatment from white landowners turned violent, resulting in a massacre where estimates of Black people killed ranged from 100 to 200.

The Slave Trade in South Carolina and the Delayed Path to Freedom

South Carolina was a central location in the transatlantic slave trade, with Charleston serving as one of the most significant entry points for enslaved Africans in North America. The economy of South Carolina depended heavily on the labor of these enslaved individuals, who were forced to work on plantations producing crops like rice, indigo, and cotton. The reality of life for these enslaved people was marked by extreme hardship, including brutal working conditions, long hours, and the constant threat of family separation due to the cruel practices of slave trading.

When the Emancipation Proclamation was issued by President Abraham Lincoln on January 1, 1863, it declared freedom for all enslaved people in Confederate-held territories. However, in practice, the proclamation had little immediate effect in places like South Carolina, where Confederate forces maintained control, and Union forces had limited influence. Many slaveholders in the state deliberately chose not to inform the enslaved people about the proclamation, hoping to retain their labor force and avoid the economic devastation that would follow the loss of free labor.

Even after the Civil War ended in April 1865, when Confederate forces surrendered, many African Americans in South Carolina and other Southern states still did not know they were free. Plantation owners, clinging to their way of life, continued to deceive their slaves, keeping them in bondage despite the legal end of slavery. This betrayal left many enslaved people toiling under the same harsh conditions, unaware that they had been granted freedom.

Juneteenth, observed on June 19th, marks the day in 1865 when Union General Gordon Granger arrived in Galveston, Texas, and announced that all enslaved people in the state were free. Texas had been a remote stronghold where slavery persisted even after the

Confederacy's defeat, and the news of emancipation took more than two years to reach the enslaved population there. Juneteenth thus symbolizes the delayed freedom that many African Americans experienced, a painful reminder that their liberation was neither swift nor fully honored when it was legally granted.

This raises a critical question: Why did it take so long for many African Americans to learn of their freedom? The delay can be attributed to a combination of geographic isolation, intentional deception by slaveholders, and the slow spread of information in the 19th century. Moreover, the deeply entrenched social and economic systems of the South were resistant to change. Plantation owners, unwilling to accept the new reality, chose to keep enslaved people in the dark, extending their suffering and exploitation.

For African Americans, Juneteenth is more than just a celebration of freedom; it is a day of reflection on the hardships and injustices that their ancestors endured. It serves as a reminder of the resilience of those who, despite the odds, ultimately emerged victorious over their oppressors. Juneteenth challenges us to consider the cost of freedom and to confront the reasons why it was withheld for so long, even after it was legally secured.

As we remember this chapter in history, it is essential to recognize the deliberate actions taken to suppress the rights of African Americans and the lasting impact these actions have had. The legacy of slavery and the prolonged path to freedom continue to influence the experiences of African Americans today. Juneteenth stands as a powerful testament to the ongoing pursuit of equality and justice in a nation still grappling with the shadows of its past.

The Scottsboro Boys Case (1931

The Scottsboro Boys case stands as one of the most infamous examples of racial injustice in the American legal system. In 1931, nine Black teenagers were falsely accused of raping two white women on a train in Alabama. The case quickly became a lightning rod for discussions about racial prejudice, the flaws of the judicial system, and the systemic oppression faced by African Americans in the South during the early 20th century.

The events that led to the Scottsboro Boys case unfolded on March 25, 1931, when a fight broke out between a group of Black and white teenagers riding a freight train through Alabama. The altercation resulted in the white youths being forced off the train, and when the train reached the town of Scottsboro, the authorities were alerted. Awaiting the train's arrival, local law enforcement officers arrested the nine Black teenagers who remained on board.

Shortly after the arrest, two white women, Ruby Bates and Victoria Price, who had also been on the train, accused the nine teenagers of raping them. These accusations, made without any substantial evidence, ignited a firestorm of racial tension. Within days, the Scottsboro Boys—ranging in age from 13 to 19—were indicted on charges of rape, a crime that carried the death penalty in Alabama.

The speed at which the legal proceedings moved forward was shocking. Despite the lack of credible evidence and the inconsistencies in the testimonies of Bates and Price, the Scottsboro Boys were quickly brought to trial in Scottsboro. In an atmosphere charged with racial hostility, the boys were provided with inadequate legal representation, and their fate seemed all but sealed.

The first set of trials, held just weeks after the arrests, resulted in the conviction of eight of the nine boys, with the jury handing down death sentences for all but the youngest, Roy Wright. The speed and outcome of these trials were widely criticized, as it became clear that the verdicts were based more on racial prejudice than on the facts of the case.

The injustice of the Scottsboro Boys' trials attracted national and international attention. Civil rights organizations, including the NAACP and the International Labor Defense (ILD), took up the case, launching an extensive campaign to secure justice for the nine teenagers. The ILD, a legal arm of the Communist Party, played a particularly crucial role in providing the Scottsboro Boys with competent legal representation and in bringing their case to the attention of the broader public.

Over the next few years, the Scottsboro Boys case became a protracted legal battle, with multiple trials and appeals. In 1932, the U.S. Supreme Court intervened in Powell v. Alabama, ruling that the Scottsboro Boys had been denied their right to adequate legal counsel, thus overturning the convictions. However, this ruling did not end the ordeal. The case was sent back to Alabama for retrial, and once again, the boys faced biased juries and hostile courtrooms.

One of the most significant developments in the case came in 1933 when Ruby Bates recanted her testimony, admitting that she and Victoria Price had fabricated the rape charges under pressure from law enforcement. Despite this admission, the Alabama courts remained determined to secure convictions, and the retrials continued to yield guilty verdicts, though not all resulted in death sentences.

The legal battles dragged on for years, and it wasn't until 1937 that four of the Scottsboro Boys—Olen Montgomery, Eugene Williams, Willie Roberson, and Roy Wright—were released after all charges against them were dropped. The other five—Clarence Norris, Charlie Weems, Andrew Wright, Ozie Powell, and Haywood Patterson—continued to face legal persecution. Some were retried, reconvicted, and sentenced to long prison terms.

The Scottsboro Boys' struggle did not end with their release from prison. The trauma of their experiences left lasting scars, and their names remained associated with a gross miscarriage of justice. Clarence Norris, the last surviving Scottsboro Boy, was eventually pardoned in 1976, more than four decades after the initial trials.

The Scottsboro Boys case highlighted the deep-seated racism that permeated the American South's legal system and underscored the urgent need for reform. It also served as a catalyst for the emerging civil rights movement, as it exposed the vulnerability of African Americans to false accusations and the often fatal consequences of racial bias in the courts.

This chapter, grounded in the facts of the case, reflects on the enduring significance of the Scottsboro Boys case as a symbol of the fight against racial injustice. Their story is a sobering reminder of the perils of prejudice and the importance of vigilance in the pursuit of true justice.

Unfortunately, not able to Trace Lineage

As an African American, I have often found myself yearning to trace my family's lineage back to the first ancestor who arrived on American soil as a slave. The quest to uncover this history is something that has weighed heavily on me, as it does on many African Americans. I often wonder, who was my family before they were enslaved? What was our true name before we were forced into the shackles of slavery in America? The lack of answers to these questions is a painful reality that many of us share.

It is heartbreaking to see other nationalities easily tracing their roots back through generations, proudly recounting the stories of their ancestors who began their family's legacy. Meanwhile, for African Americans like myself, the reality is much bleaker. Though I carry my father's name, and my father's father's name, all the way back through generations, I know that this name is not truly ours. It is a name given to us by a slave master—a constant reminder that our true heritage has been lost.

This harsh truth stings every day. Each time my name is called, I am reminded that it is not the name of my ancestors, but rather the name of the family that once owned them. For many African Americans, this realization is too painful to bear, leading some to believe that their family was never involved in the slave trade. I understand this need to distance oneself from such a painful reality, but the truth remains: if you have grandparents, and they had grandparents, you are likely connected to someone who was a victim of slavery.

Consider this: for each child born today, there are countless ancestors tied to them through the generations—ancestors who were victims of the slave trade. It's a sobering thought, realizing how many relatives you will never know, how many family members are forever lost to history. The reality of being stripped away from your past makes it easy to feel that your future is equally uncertain.

To better describe how this feels, imagine having pictures of loved ones who have passed away—precious mementos that connect you to your family's past. Now, imagine someone coming into your home, claiming to help, but instead, they throw away all those pictures. In this scenario, at least you had the chance to know the people in those photos. But for African Americans, the tragic truth is that we will never have the opportunity to know the faces of our ancestors. This reality is deeply upsetting.

African-American history has been systematically erased, leaving us to grapple with the fragments that remain. It is a harsh truth to accept, but it is a truth that we must confront if we are to understand the full impact of our lost history.

I Have Question?

PLEASE... America tell me ,was the end of the Civil War expected to bring true freedom and equality for Black Americans? seriously !!! The harsh reality is that it did not usher in a new era; instead, it led to a dark chapter in American history. Now was this period, marked by Jim Crow laws and segregation, essentially our own version of apartheid? This system of institutionalized racial segregation and discrimination was brutally enforced across the Southern states and beyond, seeking to maintain a permanent second-class status for Black people.

America tell me did Jim Crow laws represent merely a collection of oppressive regulations? No you know they didn't! , they embodied a comprehensive social order designed to keep Black people "in their place." Were these laws limited in their scope? They extended to every aspect of daily life, dictating where people could live, work, and attend school, as well as where they could sit on a bus, drink from a water fountain, or even be buried. Was racial segregation under Jim Crow limited to public spaces? It was enforced in schools, transportation, hospitals, and more, aiming to create a world where Black and white Americans lived completely separate lives, with white Americans enjoying privileges denied to Black Americans.

Was segregation just about physical separation? No, it was also about the psychological and social degradation of an entire race. Were the signs that marked "Colored" and "White" public spaces just superficial labels? They were constant reminders of inferiority, with substandard schools and neighborhoods reinforcing the message that Black people were unwelcome in white society. Was this status quo easily challenged? Any attempt to challenge it would be met with brutal force.

Was violence a distant threat under Jim Crow? No, it was ever-present, with lynching becoming a tool of terror used to enforce racial subordination. Did local authorities condone these acts of violence? Often, they did, either tacitly or explicitly. Were these lynchings rare, isolated incidents? Thousands of Black men, women, and children were lynched across the South between the late 19th and mid-20th centuries, serving as horrific spectacles meant to instill fear and maintain white supremacy. Were these lynchings just physical acts of violence? Their brutality, often conducted in public, was a grim reminder of the deadly consequences of challenging the racial order.

Was segregation only a Southern phenomenon? While it was most intensely felt in the South, segregation was a national issue. Did practices like redlining and discriminatory hiring only affect the South? No, they were prevalent across the nation, ensuring that Black Americans remained economically and socially marginalized. Was the North free from segregation? Even in Northern cities, where Jim Crow laws were not formally codified, segregation was enforced through subtle but equally devastating means. Did this lead to a racially united nation? The result was a nation deeply divided along racial lines, with inequalities that still affect American society today.

Was the psychological toll of Jim Crow on Black Americans minor? It was profound, as living under a system that constantly dehumanized and degraded them fostered a deep sense of distrust and alienation from the very nation that promised them freedom. Did the dream of equality feel real to those living under Jim Crow? It seemed like a cruel joke compared to the harsh realities they faced.

Did Black Americans simply accept their oppression? No, they resisted, forming their own communities, building their own schools, and creating cultural institutions that celebrated Black identity and resilience. Did any leaders emerge from these communities? Yes, leaders who would later spearhead the Civil Rights Movement, challenging the system of segregation and demanding the rights denied to their people for generations.

I very interested in knowing was Jim Crow only a Southern problem or a relic of the past? let me stop you , I"ll answer that for you Nooooo!, it was an integral part of the national fabric, shaping the social, economic, and political landscape of America. Believe it or not but the impact is still felt today? Absolutely, as the deep-rooted inequalities created during this period continue to influence American society. You know all this was wrong no matter what and truthfully there is no way to explain any of this , seriously! but you still have some explaining to do!

Brown v. Board of Education (1954)

The landmark case of Brown v. Board of Education of Topeka, decided by the U.S. Supreme Court in 1954, is widely regarded as one of the most significant judicial decisions in American history. This case fundamentally challenged the doctrine of "separate but equal," which had been established by the 1896 Supreme Court decision in Plessy v. Ferguson and had been used to justify racial segregation in public facilities, including schools.

The roots of Brown v. Board of Education lay in the lived experiences of African American families who were forced to send their children to segregated schools that were often underfunded and inferior in quality compared to schools for white children. In the early 1950s, several parents across different states, including Kansas, Virginia, South Carolina, Delaware, and Washington, D.C., filed lawsuits against their local school boards, challenging the constitutionality of segregated schools. These cases were eventually consolidated under the title Brown v. Board of Education, named after Oliver Brown, a parent in Topeka, Kansas, who was the first listed plaintiff.

Oliver Brown had tried to enroll his daughter, Linda Brown, in a white elementary school closer to their home, but she was denied admission due to her race. The NAACP (National Association for the Advancement of Colored People) Legal Defense and Educational Fund, led by Thurgood Marshall, took up the case, arguing that segregation violated the Equal Protection Clause of the 14th Amendment, which guarantees that no state shall deny any person within its jurisdiction the equal protection of the laws.

The NAACP's legal team presented a compelling case, highlighting the psychological effects of segregation on African American children. They used social science research, including the famous "doll test" conducted by psychologists Kenneth and Mamie Clark, which showed that segregation fostered a sense of inferiority among Black children. This evidence demonstrated that "separate but equal" facilities were inherently unequal, as segregation instilled and perpetuated feelings of racial inferiority.

On May 17, 1954, the U.S. Supreme Court, led by Chief Justice Earl Warren, issued a unanimous decision in favor of the plaintiffs. The Court declared that racial segregation in public schools was unconstitutional, stating that "separate educational facilities are inherently unequal." The decision emphasized that segregation deprived African American children of the equal protection of the laws guaranteed by the 14th Amendment.

The Brown v. Board of Education decision marked a significant victory for the civil rights movement, but it also faced significant resistance, particularly in the Southern states. The Supreme Court's ruling did not specify a timeline for the desegregation of schools, leading to delays and widespread opposition. In 1955, the Court issued a follow-up decision known as Brown II, which ordered the desegregation of schools to proceed "with all deliberate speed." However, the vague language allowed for continued resistance, and it took many years of legal battles, protests, and federal intervention to enforce desegregation in some areas.

Despite the challenges and resistance, the Brown v. Board of Education decision had a profound impact on the American legal and educational systems. It overturned the precedent set by Plessy v. Ferguson and laid the foundation for the dismantling of racial segregation in all areas of public life. The case also served as a catalyst for the broader civil rights movement, inspiring activists to continue the fight for equality and justice.

The legacy of Brown v. Board of Education endures as a pivotal moment in the struggle for civil rights in the United States. It represented a rejection of institutionalized racism and set the stage for further legal and social advancements toward racial equality. The case remains a powerful reminder of the importance of challenging injustice and the role that the judiciary can play in shaping a more equitable society

The Civil Rights Movement (1950s-1960s)

The Civil Rights Movement, spanning the 1950s and 1960s, was a defining period in American history, marked by a determined and collective effort to challenge racial segregation and discrimination. This movement, rooted in the long struggle for racial equality, sought to secure the basic rights and freedoms for African Americans that were denied to them through systemic racism and institutionalized injustice.

The origins of the Civil Rights Movement can be traced back to the deep-seated inequalities that African Americans faced in the United States, particularly in the South, where Jim Crow laws enforced racial segregation in all aspects of life. These laws, which were a legacy of the post-Reconstruction era, ensured that African Americans were treated as second-class citizens, restricted from accessing the same public facilities, schools, and employment opportunities as white Americans. The movement that emerged in the mid-20th century was a response to these injustices and aimed to dismantle the legal and social barriers that upheld racial inequality.

One of the most significant events that ignited the Civil Rights Movement was the 1954 Supreme Court decision in Brown v. Board of Education. This landmark ruling declared that racial segregation in public schools was unconstitutional, overturning the earlier Plessy v. Ferguson decision that had established the "separate but equal" doctrine. The Brown decision was a major victory for civil rights activists and set the stage for further challenges to segregation and discrimination.

However, the road to equality was fraught with resistance and violence. The integration of public schools, for example, was met with fierce opposition from white segregationists. In 1957, the Little Rock Nine, a group of African American students, faced violent mobs as they attempted to integrate Central High School in Little Rock, Arkansas.

President Dwight D. Eisenhower was forced to intervene by sending federal troops to escort the students into the school, underscoring the federal government's commitment to enforcing desegregation.

The Civil Rights Movement was characterized by its use of nonviolent protest and civil disobedience, strategies that were inspired by the teachings of Mahatma Gandhi and led by prominent figures such as Martin Luther King Jr. The Montgomery Bus Boycott of 1955-1956, sparked by Rosa Parks' refusal to give up her seat to a white passenger, was one of the first major demonstrations of the power of nonviolent resistance. The boycott, which lasted for over a year, led to a Supreme Court ruling that declared segregation on public buses unconstitutional and marked a significant victory for the movement.

As the movement gained momentum, it expanded its focus to address a wide range of issues, including voting rights, employment discrimination, and police brutality. The Southern Christian Leadership Conference (SCLC), founded by King and other civil rights leaders, played a central role in organizing protests and advocating for legislative change. The sit-in movement, initiated by four African American college students at a Woolworth's lunch counter in Greensboro, North Carolina, in 1960, became a powerful tactic for challenging segregation in public spaces.

The Freedom Rides of 1961, organized by the Congress of Racial Equality (CORE), aimed to test the enforcement of Supreme Court rulings that prohibited segregation in interstate bus travel. These rides, which involved integrated groups of activists traveling through the South, were met with brutal violence from white mobs, yet they drew national attention to the persistence of segregation and the need for federal intervention.

The Civil Rights Movement reached its peak with the March on Washington for Jobs and Freedom on August 28, 1963. This historic event, which brought together over 250,000 people at the Lincoln Memorial, was a powerful demonstration of the movement's broad support and its demand for racial and economic justice. It was during this march that Martin Luther King Jr. delivered his iconic "I Have a Dream" speech, articulating a vision of a future where all people would be judged by the content of their character rather than the color of their skin.

Despite these victories, the struggle for civil rights was far from over. The movement faced significant challenges, including the violent backlash from white supremacists who sought to maintain the status quo. The bombing of the 16th Street Baptist Church in Birmingham, Alabama, in 1963, which killed four young African American girls, and the assassination of civil rights leaders such as Medgar Evers and Martin Luther King Jr., underscored the high cost of the fight for equality.

The movement's efforts culminated in the passage of landmark legislation, including the Civil Rights Act of 1964 and the Voting Rights Act of 1965. The Civil Rights Act banned discrimination based on race, color, religion, sex, or national origin and ended segregation in public places, while the Voting Rights Act aimed to eliminate barriers to voting for African Americans, particularly in the South. These laws represented significant steps forward in the pursuit of racial equality, although the struggle for justice and equity would continue in the years to come.

The legacy of the Civil Rights Movement is profound, as it not only brought about critical legal and social changes but also inspired future generations to continue the fight for human rights. The movement's emphasis on nonviolent protest, its moral clarity, and its vision of a just and inclusive society remain powerful lessons for contemporary struggles against injustice and inequality.

This chapter, rooted in original thought and historical fact, reflects on the profound impact of the Civil Rights Movement of the 1950s and 1960s, a movement that reshaped the United States and set the course for future progress in the ongoing fight for civil rights.

If Things were Done Right After Slavery

In an ideal scenario, the federal government would have implemented programs designed to empower freed slaves economically. Land redistribution could have been a priority, enabling African American families to cultivate land and establish financial independence. Such initiatives would have paved the way for a prosperous Black middle class, fostering stability and community growth.

Education as a Right

Education would have been recognized as a fundamental right for all citizens, with significant investments made in schools for African Americans. By providing equal access to quality education, future generations would have been equipped with the knowledge and skills necessary to thrive in various professional fields. This emphasis on education could have significantly altered the socio-economic landscape, allowing African Americans to challenge systemic inequalities.

Political Inclusion and Representation

A transformative post-slavery America would have seen active efforts to include African Americans in the political arena. Ensuring representation at all levels of government would have empowered African Americans to advocate for policies addressing their unique challenges. A robust political presence would have led to legislation focused on equity and justice, reinforcing the principles of democracy.

Fostering Social Integration

Instead of the segregation that became prevalent during the Reconstruction era, a commitment to social integration could have been championed. Initiatives promoting collaboration between Black and white communities would have built understanding and reduced racial tensions. Emphasizing shared experiences and cultural exchange could have enriched the nation's identity, fostering a more inclusive society.

Embracing Restorative Justice

The legacy of slavery could have been addressed through a focus on restorative justice, fostering national conversations about the injustices endured by African Americans. Acknowledgment, apologies, and reparations would have honored the dignity of those affected, creating pathways for healing. This approach would have recognized the past while working toward a more just future.

Cultural Renaissance and Recognition

The post-slavery period could have ignited a cultural renaissance, celebrating the profound contributions of African Americans to art, music, and literature. Freed from systemic oppression, African American voices could have thrived, shaping the cultural landscape of the nation. Acknowledging these contributions would have woven a rich tapestry of history, reflecting the diversity of American identity

Disrespect and Neglect Among African Americans Burial Practices

Throughout history, the treatment of African Americans extended beyond the living; it permeated into the realm of death and remembrance. The burial practices for Black individuals, especially in the post-Civil War era and throughout the Jim Crow period, were often marked by a profound disrespect that mirrored the dehumanization they faced in life. This disrespect manifested most starkly in the neglect of burial sites, where many African Americans were laid to rest without the dignity of proper memorialization.

In many communities, cemeteries designated for African Americans were often poorly maintained or entirely neglected. While white cemeteries received care and attention, Black burial sites were left to deteriorate, with overgrown weeds, broken fences, and unmarked graves. This stark contrast was not just a matter of aesthetics; it was a reflection of the deep-seated racism that permeated every aspect of life, including death. The lack of resources allocated to these cemeteries spoke volumes about the societal belief that African American lives—and by extension, deaths—were of lesser value.

The absence of headstones over the graves of African Americans was particularly telling. Many families were unable to afford the cost of a proper headstone, while others were denied the opportunity altogether due to systemic discrimination. In some cases, even when families wanted to commemorate their loved ones with a headstone, local regulations or societal attitudes made it nearly impossible. This resulted in countless graves marked only by simple wooden crosses or, in many instances, left entirely unmarked, erasing the identities of those who had passed.

The impact of this neglect extends beyond the physical absence of headstones. It signifies a deeper societal disregard for the humanity and history of African Americans. The failure to recognize and honor the resting places of Black individuals is akin to a continued erasure of their existence and contributions to society. Each unmarked grave represents not just an individual lost but a history that remains unacknowledged.

Moreover, the disrespect shown in burial practices often exacerbated the grief of families. In communities where mourning was already fraught with trauma—due to violence, systemic poverty, and loss—having to bury a loved one without proper acknowledgment only compounded the pain. Families were left to navigate their sorrow in spaces that felt devoid of dignity and respect, further alienating them from the very act of remembering their loved ones.

In contemporary times, many African American communities have begun to reclaim their burial sites, advocating for the recognition and restoration of neglected cemeteries. Organizations dedicated to preserving African American history and culture are working to document these burial sites, ensuring that the stories of those who have been forgotten are told and remembered. Community efforts to erect headstones and memorials serve as powerful acts of reclamation, transforming spaces of neglect into places of honor and remembrance.

This movement toward restoration is a critical step in addressing the historical injustices faced by African Americans in life and death. It represents a broader desire to reclaim dignity, respect, and agency over their narratives. By honoring the resting places of their ancestors, communities can begin to heal from the wounds of the past and create a legacy that affirms their humanity.

As we reflect on the treatment of African Americans regarding burial practices, it is essential to recognize the profound disrespect that has been inflicted upon them. The lack of headstones, care for burial sites, and acknowledgment of their lives is a reminder of the broader systemic issues of racism and dehumanization that continue to persist.

By confronting this history, we can honor the memories of those who came before and work toward a future where all lives—both lived and lost—are respected and valued.

This chapter addresses the historical disrespect shown to African Americans in burial practices, focusing on the lack of headstones and proper memorialization, while also highlighting efforts to reclaim and honor these burial sites today.

Mental State of the African American

It takes a mental toll to endure prejudice from a young age. As an African American, I learned that I must navigate in a world where I am often judged by my skin and not my character. Unfortunately, I'm always forced to face the fact that there's a possibility I might not make it home because of being Black in America—being in the wrong place at the wrong time, making the wrong move at the wrong time, or being stopped by the police. All of this plays a factor in the reality of how society is.

Unfortunately, a collective events of police brutality has been conducted from the beginning of the African Americans experience the psychological aspects of racism has left a strain on the African-American, every story about a victim demise by the hands of law-enforcement due to negligence as calls, more protesting, and rioting for equal rights. Some would like to classified as poor training in the police department, but the facts are what the reality is showing is pure hate for the African-American no matter what you do, you could follow the orders of the officer but they'll find a way to use a lethal force, and get away with it by saying they felt threatened.

As we reflect on the mental state of African Americans in America today, we must understand that the fight against prejudice is not just a personal battle, but a collective one. It is a call to action for all of us to stand against injustice, to listen, to learn, and to work together to create a society where everyone is truly equal—where the weight of injustice is finally lifted, and every person is free to live without fear of a victim

I think about my wife, my five sisters, my mother, and my mother-in-law, and all the things they have to go through now in society with the stereotypes. I thank God that they are not in the world that our ancestors had to suffer through. Throughout history, Black women had to be subjected to malicious events. It was believed that the African woman possessed an extraordinary capacity to endure pain. This stereotype enabled many horrible events, mistreating and harming African women both physically, mentally, and emotionally. No matter how many times during a procedure in their experiments, they didn't care how long she screamed. The African woman was raped, forced against her will to do things that only she would do with her husband. She was forced to bear children, breeding them just for enslavement. There was no love, just brutal violence.

All of this was meant to break the African woman. The emotional and psychological toll is embedded in the blood, passed down from generation to generation, coded in the DNA.

Every group of people experiencing slavery is a devastating situation, no matter their religion, background, or race. The humanity of the situation should always focus on the many topics concerning people being enslaved. However, this book was specifically written for African Americans and their struggles. I encourage you to do more research into the history of African Americans, whether you share the same race or not. There are many topics I didn't touch on in this book that I am preserving for the next one.

But it's crucial to understand the mind of the enslaved and all the challenges that had to be overcome—the misery, agony, and pain of going to a different land that was foreign, being forced to change your name, being split up from your family. And ever since then, things haven't truly changed. The African mind has been programmed, still stuck in whips and chains.

The Tragic Destruction of Black Wall Street

One hundred years ago, in the early 20th century, a thriving African-American community known as Black Wall Street existed in the Greenwood District of Tulsa, Oklahoma. This community was one of the most prosperous African-American enclaves in the United States, filled with Black-owned businesses, including banks, theaters, law offices, and schools. African Americans in Greenwood had built a self-sustaining economy, demonstrating remarkable independence and entrepreneurial spirit.

During this time, African Americans in Greenwood were achieving significant economic success, generating wealth that was rare for Black communities in America due to systemic oppression and racism. Their businesses thrived without the need for assistance from white Americans, showcasing that they could achieve financial independence on their own. This success fostered a sense of pride and self-reliance within the community but also stirred envy and resentment among many white Americans in the area.

The mere existence of a wealthy, self-sufficient Black community contradicted the prevailing racist ideologies of the time, which held that African Americans were inherently inferior and incapable of such achievements. The prosperity of Greenwood posed a direct challenge to these racist beliefs, fueling anger and resentment among white residents who felt threatened by the success of their Black neighbors. The idea that African Americans could prosper without the help of white people was deeply unsettling to those who had long considered themselves superior.

The racial tension in Tulsa reached a boiling point on May 31, 1921, when a young Black man, Dick Rowland, was accused of assaulting a white woman, Sarah Page, in an elevator. Although the details of the incident remain unclear, the accusation alone was enough to ignite a violent response. Rumors spread quickly, inflaming the already tense atmosphere, and a white mob began to form, seeking to take justice into their own hands by lynching Rowland.

When African-American men from Greenwood, many of whom were World War I veterans, arrived at the courthouse to protect Rowland, tensions escalated. The white mob, feeling emboldened and enraged by the sight of armed Black men, began a full-scale attack on the Greenwood District. Over the next 24 hours, the mob, numbering in the thousands, unleashed a horrific wave of violence, looting, and arson upon the community.

White rioters, armed with guns and even incendiary bombs dropped from private planes, set fire to Black-owned homes and businesses, reducing the once-thriving neighborhood to ashes. The destruction was systematic and brutal, leaving nearly 1,200 buildings destroyed and hundreds of Black residents dead. Those who survived were left homeless and destitute, their dreams and livelihoods shattered in an instant.

The attack on Black Wall Street was motivated by a toxic mix of racism, jealousy, and a desire to maintain the status quo of white supremacy. The success of Greenwood's Black residents represented a threat to the racial and economic hierarchies that white society had long imposed. The idea that African Americans could build wealth and independence on their own was unacceptable to those who believed that Black people should remain subservient and dependent on white people for their livelihood.

The Greenwood massacre was not just an act of violence; it was a calculated attempt to erase a symbol of Black excellence and independence. The white mob's actions were driven by a fear that if African Americans could succeed on their own, they might begin to challenge the broader systems of oppression that kept them marginalized. By destroying Black Wall Street, the rioters sought to send a clear message that any attempt by African Americans to achieve economic or social autonomy would be met with brutal force.

For centuries, African Americans have demonstrated extraordinary strength, determination, and work ethic, often under the harshest conditions imaginable. From the brutal era of slavery, where Black people were forced to labor tirelessly without any compensation or recognition, to the rise of thriving Black communities like Black Wall Street, the history of African Americans is a testament to perseverance and entrepreneurial spirit.

Despite the systemic barriers designed to keep them oppressed, African Americans have consistently contributed to the building and prosperity of the United States. The wealth generated by their labor during slavery laid the economic foundation of the nation, and after emancipation, African Americans continued to work hard to carve out spaces of success, even in the face of overwhelming odds.

The destruction of Black Wall Street in Tulsa, Oklahoma, is a tragic example of how Black success was met with violence and jealousy. Before the massacre, this community was a beacon of African American achievement, with Black-owned businesses, banks, and other establishments flourishing. This wasn't an anomaly but a reflection of what African Americans could accomplish when given the opportunity to thrive. The massacre didn't just destroy buildings; it was an attempt to crush the spirit of a people who had proven time and again that they were far from lazy—they were industrious, resourceful, and determined.

Even today, African Americans continue to be some of the hardest-working individuals in the country. The systemic challenges may have evolved, but the resilience remains. Whether it's in the workplace, in entrepreneurship, or in the ongoing fight for equality and justice, African Americans are not only working hard—they are excelling and pushing the boundaries of what is possible.

It's crucial that this reality is recognized and respected. The narrative must change, and it must reflect the truth: African Americans are, and always have been, among the hardest-working people in this country. The legacy of slavery, followed by decades of discrimination, has not diminished this fact; rather, it has highlighted the extraordinary resilience of a people who continue to contribute significantly to the fabric of American society.

The timeline of history is indeed relevant. Slavery was not that long ago, and its repercussions are still felt today. It's time for a collective acknowledgment of this truth and for the harmful stereotypes to be replaced with the recognition of African American strength, ingenuity, and work ethic. Only then can the healing begin, and only then can we truly move forward as a society that values and honors the contributions of all its members

In the aftermath of the massacre, the survivors of Greenwood faced immense challenges in rebuilding their lives. Despite their resilience and determination, the loss of wealth, property, and community had a lasting impact. The destruction of Black Wall Street served as a grim reminder of the lengths to which white society would go to maintain its dominance and suppress Black progress.

It's important to note that the events of Black Wall Street and its destruction are part of the public domain, meaning they are well-documented historical facts. Because these events are public knowledge and are not owned by any individual or entity, they can be discussed openly in this book. This information is not subject to copyright protection, and discussing it here does not pose any legal risks related to defamation or intellectual property. By writing about Black Wall Street, I am honoring the memory of those who suffered and ensuring that this critical piece of history is never forgotten.

Which should've been done after the Black Wall Street massacre

In the wake of the massacre, there should have been a collective recognition of the atrocities committed against the Black residents of Greenwood. Instead of the silence that followed, a robust system of accountability should have been established. Those responsible for the violence—the armed mobs, the law enforcement officials who stood by, and the individuals who incited the violence—should have faced swift justice. Incarceration for the perpetrators would not only have served as a deterrent for future acts of racial violence but would also have acknowledged the gravity of their actions. It is essential to understand that justice is not merely about punishment; it is also about validating the experiences of the victims and their families.

The families of those who were murdered or displaced during the massacre deserved reparations for their suffering. Financial support could have taken many forms, including direct compensation for lost lives, property, and businesses. The destruction of Black Wall Street represented not only the loss of homes but also the obliteration of dreams and aspirations. Survivors should have been granted funds to help them rebuild their lives, allowing them to restore their sense of dignity and agency.

Additionally, the establishment of community development programs aimed at fostering economic growth in the wake of the tragedy would have been essential. Such programs could have provided resources and training for survivors, helping them to establish new businesses and create employment opportunities within the community. By investing in the resilience of Black Wall Street, the government could have played a critical role in ensuring that the legacy of Greenwood lived on, rather than being buried beneath the rubble of violence and hatred.

Educational initiatives should also have been prioritized for the survivors and their descendants. Understanding the history of Black Wall Street and the events that transpired would have allowed future generations to honor their ancestors and draw strength from their resilience. Educational scholarships and programs aimed at empowering young Black individuals would have fostered a sense of pride and purpose, creating leaders who could advocate for justice and equality.

Moreover, the national acknowledgment of the Greenwood Massacre should have been a priority. Public memorials, historical sites, and educational campaigns could have served to inform the broader public about the significance of Black Wall Street and the ongoing impact of systemic racism. Recognizing the tragedy in a meaningful way would have not only honored the victims but also encouraged conversations about racial justice and the need for reparative measures.

The survivors of Black Wall Street faced a long, painful road to healing, a journey made more difficult by the lack of support from the government and society at large. What should have happened in the aftermath of the massacre was a concerted effort to provide justice, financial support, and community rebuilding initiatives. By taking these steps, we could have honored the legacy of Black Wall Street, affirming the resilience of its residents and ensuring that the lessons of the past are not forgotten.

Ultimately, the events of 1921 serve as a powerful reminder of the importance of justice, accountability, and healing in the face of tragedy. For the survivors of Black Wall Street, there should have been not only recognition of their suffering but also tangible support that would allow them to reclaim their lives and their community. As we reflect on this dark chapter in American history, let us strive to ensure that the stories of resilience and strength are honored and that the fight for justice continues.

Symbol of Racial Terror

The Ku Klux Klan (KKK) emerged in the aftermath of the Civil War as a violent response to the newfound freedoms of African Americans. Founded in 1865, the Klan quickly became a symbol of racial terror, employing intimidation, violence, and murder to maintain white supremacy and resist the civil rights of Black individuals. The Klan's reign of terror included lynchings, arson, and the destruction of Black communities, creating a climate of fear that reverberated throughout the South and beyond.

The KKK was not just a fringe group; it infiltrated various institutions, including law enforcement and even the medical community. In many towns, local police forces were complicit in Klan activities, turning a blind eye to the violence or, in some cases, actively participating in it. The very officers sworn to protect the citizens often aligned themselves with the Klan's ideology, reinforcing a system of oppression that made African Americans feel unsafe in their own neighborhoods.

This betrayal was not limited to law enforcement. Many individuals who held respectable positions in society—such as doctors, lawyers, and politicians—were also associated with the Klan or harbored its beliefs. In their roles, they often perpetuated discriminatory practices, treating African Americans with disdain or outright hostility. This duality of being both a respected member of society and an enforcer of racial terror created a complicated and painful reality for Black individuals seeking care, justice, or simply the dignity they deserved.

The consequences of this systemic betrayal were dire. African Americans faced immense obstacles when seeking healthcare, as many physicians refused to treat them or provided substandard care. This mistrust in the medical community has had lasting effects, contributing to ongoing disparities in health outcomes and access to quality care. The legacy of fear and discrimination left an indelible mark on the relationship between Black communities and those in positions of authority, whether in law enforcement or medicine.

The psychological impact of this betrayal runs deep. For generations, African Americans have been forced to navigate a society where those sworn to protect and serve often view them through a lens of suspicion and hostility. The Klan's legacy of terror created a pervasive environment of mistrust, where seeking help from authorities or medical professionals could lead to further harm rather than support.

Yet, despite the trauma inflicted by the KKK and its affiliates, the resilience of the African American community has shone through. Grassroots movements, civil rights organizations, and community leaders have worked tirelessly to combat the legacies of hate and violence. Advocacy for police reform, equitable healthcare access, and systemic change has become central to the ongoing struggle for justice and equality.

As we reflect on this dark chapter in American history, it is crucial to acknowledge the ways in which the KKK's influence has shaped societal structures and relationships. Understanding this legacy allows us to confront the realities of systemic racism that persist today and to work towards building a future where all individuals, regardless of their race, can access justice, care, and dignity.

The journey toward healing and reconciliation is ongoing, requiring a collective effort to dismantle the systems that have perpetuated violence and discrimination. By confronting the painful truths of the past, we can forge a path toward a more equitable society, ensuring that the legacy of the KKK does not define the future of African Americans or the nation as a whole.

The Evolving Face of the Ku Klux Klan: A Legacy of Terror and Modern-Day Manifestations

The Ku Klux Klan (KKK) has a long history of destroying African-American families and communities through acts of terror.

In the dark days of the past, they were easily recognizable by their white sheets and hoods as they rode horses through neighborhoods, spreading fear and chaos. These night riders would set fires, often burning crosses on the lands of African-American families, all in an attempt to provoke a war—a war they knew would result in the deaths of thousands of African Americans. Their goal was simple: to maintain a stranglehold on power by any means necessary, even if it meant committing acts of unspeakable violence.

Over the years, however, the Klan has evolved. No longer do they openly wear the white sheets that once signaled their presence. Today, their uniforms have changed, but their intentions remain as sinister as ever. The modern-day Klan operates within the structures of society, often donning the uniforms of professional careers that bring them into daily contact with African Americans. This makes their mission of inflicting harm even more insidious, as they use their positions to carry out their evil plans under the guise of legitimacy.

In the medical field, for instance, some doctors, who may harbor racist beliefs, might not give the same level of care to African-American patients as they would to others. These individuals may enter the room already resigned to signing a death certificate, rather than fighting to save a life. The patient's skin color becomes a factor in the care they receive, or rather, the care they are denied.

Law enforcement is another arena where the modern-day Klan operates. There are situations where police officers, when dealing with African Americans, resort to deadly force unnecessarily. These officers approach situations with preconceived notions, already having decided that the African-American individual before them is a threat. This mindset often leads to tragic outcomes, where excessive force is used, and lives are lost. The same applies within the judicial system, where judges may hand down harsher sentences to African-American defendants than they would to their Caucasian counterparts, effectively "throwing the book" at them in a show of systemic bias.

Across the board, there are calculated moves being made to keep African Americans in check, akin to a game of chess where every piece is positioned to lead to a checkmate. The Klan may have changed its appearance, but the game remains the same—one where the stakes are the lives and futures of African Americans.

This chapter serves as a reminder that while the faces and methods may have evolved, the underlying intent of racial oppression persists. It is crucial for readers to understand the depth of this issue and recognize the modern-day manifestations of the Klan's ideology in various sectors of society. Only through awareness and active resistance can the cycle of hate and oppression be broken.

My Grandparents

My family on my father's side originally moved from South Carolina to Philadelphia in 1950. At the time, my grandparents were in their twenties, and my father was only thirteen years old. I grew up hearing stories about what life was like in South Carolina, and I've always been curious about why they decided to move to Philadelphia. South Carolina offered more land, more space, and the potential for a larger home compared to what Philadelphia had to offer in those days. So, why leave all that behind?

My grandparents lived long lives, passing away in their nineties, and I find myself wishing I had asked them the hard questions—the real questions—about their experiences in South Carolina and the history that shaped their lives and those of their parents. If my grandparents were in their nineties when they passed, and slavery ended 159 years ago, it's likely that their parents were children around the time when slavery was abolished. This timeline gives me a lot to think about.

It's a sobering thought to consider how close my family history is to such a dark period in American history. The fact that I am only a couple of generations removed from slavery is a stark reminder of how recent it was. Yet, I also recognize how fortunate I am to have been born in the generation that I am in—a time far removed from the struggles and hardships that my ancestors endured. This reflection on the timeline of my family's history gives me a deeper appreciation for the sacrifices they made and the resilience they showed in the face of unimaginable adversity. It also leaves me with a sense of responsibility to honor their legacy by continuing to ask the hard questions, even when the answers may be difficult to hear

As a child, I didn't fully understand the weight of these stories. But as I grew older, I realized that the experiences of my ancestors were not just family lore; they were part of a larger narrative that shaped the lives of millions of African Americans. This realization came into sharper focus when I discovered the slave narratives from the Federal Writers' Project.

These narratives, collected during the 1930s, offer a window into the lives of those who endured the unimaginable. They are the voices of men and women who were born into slavery, who lived through its horrors, and who somehow found the strength to share their stories. As I read through these accounts, I couldn't help but draw parallels between their experiences and the stories my grandparents had told me.

One narrative, in particular, struck a chord with me. It was the story of a man named John, who, like my grandparents, had migrated from the South to the North in search of a better life. John spoke of the struggle to hold on to his dignity in a world that sought to strip him of it at every turn. His words resonated with me because they echoed the struggles my own family faced—struggles that, though different in time and place, were rooted in the same systemic injustices.

In writing this chapter, I want to connect my family's story to the broader history of African Americans. The slave narratives are more than just historical documents; they are a testament to the resilience of a people who refused to be silenced. By weaving together the personal and the historical, I hope to honor the legacy of my ancestors and contribute to the ongoing conversation about race, identity, and justice in America.

The Story of John

John was born in the heart of Georgia in 1842, on a plantation where the fields seemed to stretch out endlessly under the Southern sun. His earliest memories were of his mother, her hands rough from picking cotton, and her voice soft as she hummed the old spirituals that had been passed down through generations. John's father had been sold when he was just a baby, a ghost in his memory, mentioned only in the quiet moments of the night when his mother thought he was asleep.

As a child, John quickly learned the ways of the plantation. The overseer's whip was never far, and the fear of it drove him to work harder and faster, though his small hands ached and his back bent under the weight of the cotton sack. But there were moments of reprieve—times when the older slaves would gather around the fire after the day's work was done, telling stories of freedom, of lands far away where no man could own another. These stories filled John's heart with a longing that he couldn't yet name.

The Emancipation Proclamation came when John was just 21 years old, but freedom did not come quickly to the plantation. The news of Lincoln's decree was kept from them, hidden by the master who feared losing his workforce. It wasn't until Union soldiers came through the area, two years later, that John finally learned he was a free man.

Freedom was not what John had imagined. With no land, no money, and little more than the clothes on his back, he set out on foot, heading north. He followed the stories he had heard in whispers—of cities where a Black man could earn an honest living, where he could be something more than what he had been born into.

John found himself in Philadelphia, a city bustling with opportunity but also fraught with its own challenges. The streets were crowded, and the work was hard to come by. But John was determined. He took on any job he could find—hauling goods at the docks, sweeping streets, even working in the foundries where the heat was as relentless as the Georgia sun. It was grueling work, but it was work he chose, and that made all the difference.

As the years passed, John built a life for himself. He married a woman named Sarah, who had also come north seeking freedom, and together they had three children. They lived in a small but sturdy house in a neighborhood filled with others who had made the same journey. They formed a community, bound together by their shared experiences and their hopes for a better future.

But the scars of slavery never fully faded. John often found himself thinking back to the plantation, to the family he had left behind, to the father he had never known. He carried those memories with him always, a reminder of where he had come from and how far he had come.

In the evenings, John would sit on his porch, his grandchildren playing at his feet, and he would tell them stories—stories of a time when men were not free, when their ancestors had been forced to work the land under the lash of the overseer's whip. But he also told them stories of hope, of resilience, of the strength it took to survive and the courage it took to seek freedom. He wanted them to know their history, to understand the sacrifices that had been made so that they could live a life free from the chains that had once bound their people.

John lived to see the turn of the century, an old man by then, with gray hair and a stooped back. But even in his final days, he held his head high, proud of the life he had made, proud of the legacy he would leave behind. For John knew that though he had been born a slave, he had lived as a free man, and that was something no one could ever take away from him.

Racism is Taught

I don't believe that anyone is born racist. Racism is something that has to be taught, passed down through generations, often by parents or other family members. Have you ever watched children playing together? They don't see color; they only care about the toys they're playing with. I've seen this with my own children on the playground. They play with kids of all colors, and there's no sign of prejudice. They share the swings, the monkey bars, the slide—just being kids.

It's usually the parents who intervene when a child gets too close to becoming too friendly with a Black child. They quickly grab their child and say, "Okay, it's time to go." I've witnessed this on two occasions, and it bothered me deeply because my son didn't understand why, but I did.

I have many friends who are Caucasian, and they often tell me that they have relatives who wouldn't be okay with them having an African American friend because of their upbringing. They always assure me that they are nothing like their relatives—that they are nowhere near racist.

The first thing I tell them is that I appreciate their honesty, and I'm glad they don't judge people by the color of their skin, but by their character. It's important to appreciate those who understand and want to help make a change.

I think about the many Caucasians who stood by Martin Luther King Jr. during his marches and were victimized alongside African Americans. That has to be one of the greatest examples of standing by your neighbor, especially when you could easily be a bystander, a sayer rather than a doer. To stand by your brother in faith for what you know is right is one of the most honorable things a person can do.

What I see lacking in today's society is a lot of our Caucasian brothers standing up for what is right, not just standing by and watching. I want to acknowledge the fact that, throughout history, there have been non-Black Americans who stood up for the rights of African Americans during slavery and afterward. This is what separates true believers in Christ from those who just use the Bible to benefit themselves and justify the enslavement of others.

Understanding Perspectives: A Chapter on Compassion and Unity

In my journey of understanding race and the complex emotions tied to it, I've come to realize that not every Caucasian is inherently racist. It's essential to acknowledge that anyone, regardless of skin color, can find themselves on either side of the fence—whether it be holding prejudiced views or standing firmly against them. Life experiences shape our perspectives, and those experiences can sometimes lead to misguided beliefs.

I recall a conversation I had with a Caucasian man at work, which I deeply appreciated for its raw honesty. He shared with me a time in his life when he was attacked by two African American men. This violent encounter left him scared, hurt, and, at that moment, filled with hatred toward African Americans. He admitted that his feelings were rooted in the trauma of that experience rather than an ingrained belief. It was not natural to him to harbor such hatred—it grew out of fear and the pain of being violated. He explained that the actions of those two men, whom he viewed as representatives of the African American race, tainted his view of the entire community for a time.

As we talked, I expressed my understanding of his feelings, though I also challenged him to see things from a different perspective. I asked him to imagine, for a moment, the roles reversed. To picture his own race being subjected to the atrocities of being slaughtered, snatched from their homeland, and then, after centuries of suffering, asked to forgive. I asked him to consider the pain of constantly being reminded by society that, despite the progress, the color of one's skin still invites prejudice and discrimination. He listened and understood the parallel I was drawing, and he shared that he no longer held those feelings of hatred. His experience was born out of a dark time, but it did not define who he became.

This conversation reinforced my belief that our experiences profoundly affect how we view the world and those around us. The fear and hatred he felt after his traumatic encounter are, in many ways, similar to the fear and resentment African Americans feel after experiencing racial acts against them. The key to overcoming these emotions lies in recognizing that there are bad apples in every tree, regardless of nationality. It's up to each of us to discern the character of the individuals we interact with, rather than judge them by their skin color.

It's crucial that we do not contribute to the creation of monsters—people who develop a deep-seated hatred for a race based on the actions of a few. We all have a responsibility to ensure that our actions do not reflect poorly on the communities we come from. Whether Black or White, our actions can either reinforce negative stereotypes or help to dismantle them.

America, SAY HIS NAME, TILL!

In 1955, a tragic event involving Emmett Till, a 14-year-old African American boy, occurred in Money, Mississippi. While visiting family, Till was accused of offending a white woman named Carolyn Bryant in her family's grocery store. The details surrounding this accusation are unclear, reflecting the deep-seated racial tensions that permeated the Jim Crow South, a time marked by widespread segregation and discrimination.

After the alleged incident, Till was kidnapped by Roy Bryant, Carolyn's husband, and his half-brother, J.W. Milam. They subjected him to a brutal attack before murdering him and disposing of his body in the Tallahatchie River. His remains were found days later, severely disfigured and unrecognizable. Despite the shocking nature of the crime, there was a disturbing delay in bringing the offenders to justice.

Mamie Till-Mobley, Emmett's mother, showed remarkable courage by opting for an open-casket funeral for her son. This decision allowed the public to witness the brutal reality of racial violence. Graphic images of Till's mutilated body appeared in newspapers and magazines, stirring outrage and grief across the nation. His funeral became a significant moment in the civil rights movement, illustrating the severe violence faced by African Americans.

The trial of Roy Bryant and J.W. Milam drew significant media attention. Even with compelling evidence against them, the all-white jury acquitted the men after a mere 67 minutes of deliberation. This outcome highlighted the entrenched systemic racism in the Southern legal system, deepening the discontent and frustration among civil rights advocates.

Emmett Till's murder and the ensuing trial marked a critical turning point for the civil rights movement. His story motivated activists and organizations, such as the NAACP, to combat racial injustice and violence, underscoring the pressing need for change in a society riddled with discrimination.

The legacy of Emmett Till continues to be relevant today, serving as a poignant reminder of the devastating effects of racial hatred. His story encourages ongoing efforts to confront systemic injustices and promote equality, urging each of us to consider our roles in advancing human rights.

In honoring Emmett Till, we are reminded of the importance of taking action against injustice, commemorating his memory, and ensuring that the lessons of our past are not forgotten. By doing so, we contribute to the ongoing pursuit of a society where every individual is treated with respect and dignity.

Growing up in one of Philadelphia's most violent neighborhoods, where gunfire was a frequent sound, there was one principle that stood unchallenged: the protection of women and children. Even in the most dangerous projects, this unwritten rule was respected. Harm to women and children was off-limits. It was a street moral code, held by some of the most dangerous individuals in the city. Violating this rule was met with swift and often severe consequences, as the streets had their own way of handling such transgressions.

I do not condone violence, yet I understand that under certain circumstances, the community felt it necessary to uphold these codes. However, what happened to Emmett Till was a gross violation of any moral code. He was an innocent boy, unaware of the malevolence that lurked in the town he visited. The people in that town knew he was not from there, and they took advantage of his naivety.

The tragedy of Emmett Till was not just a failure of justice; it was a failure of humanity. The town stood by and allowed it to happen, and America, as it has done too often, made excuses for its conduct. The brutal murder of Emmett Till is just one of many incidents that highlight the deep-rooted racism and cruelty in this country. It is a story that continues to break my heart.

The fact that a mother had to bury her son in such a horrific way is unbearable. But Emmett Till's mother, Mamie Till-Mobley, showed an unimaginable strength in the face of this tragedy. She knew that something had to be done to force America to confront its wrongs. By choosing to have an open casket funeral, she made sure that the world could see what was done to her son. Her courage ensured that Emmett Till's death was not in vain and that his story would be a catalyst for change.

What happened to Emmett Till should never have happened, and it should never happen again. As I reflect on this, I am filled with a deep sense of sorrow and anger. Yet, I also find myself in awe of the strength displayed by those who, even in the face of such unimaginable pain, chose to stand up and demand justice. This chapter is a testament to the power of truth and the enduring fight for justice in the face of overwhelming darkness.

We should've happen After Till

Imagine a world where the legal system took a firm stance against false accusations that perpetuated racial violence. In this scenario, Carolyn Bryant would have been held accountable for her role in instigating the tragedy. Instead of being allowed to walk free, she would face serious legal consequences for lying about Emmett Till. By locking her up, society would send a clear message that fabricating stories that lead to violence would not be tolerated.

2. The Death Penalty for the Murderers

In this alternate reality, the men responsible for Emmett's murder, J.W. Milam and Roy Bryant, would not have escaped justice. Following their capture, they would face a trial that prioritized the truth and sought justice for Till. With overwhelming evidence and public outcry demanding accountability, the jury would deliver a swift verdict—guilty of murder. The state, recognizing the heinous nature of their crime, would impose the death penalty, sending shockwaves through the community.

3. A Nation Confronting Its Conscience

The swift and decisive action taken against those responsible for Emmett Till's death would have catalyzed a national reckoning. A society grappling with the reality of its racism would be compelled to confront its past and reassess its values. This could have ignited a movement demanding accountability for racial violence, leading to broader discussions about justice, equality, and the need for systemic reform.

4. Strengthening the Civil Rights Movement

With a clear example of accountability, the civil rights movement would gain momentum. Activists and community leaders could leverage the outcome of Till's case to advocate for meaningful change. The message would resonate: justice for Black lives is not just an aspiration but a legal and moral imperative. This could inspire further actions aimed at dismantling systemic racism and fighting for equality.

5. Changing the Narrative Around Racial Violence

The aftermath of this scenario would alter the narrative surrounding racial violence in America. Instead of a tragic tale of injustice, the story of Emmett Till would become one of hope and accountability. The legal repercussions faced by those who perpetuated violence would encourage communities to demand justice rather than accept it as an unfortunate norm. This shift could empower future generations to stand against injustice, fostering a culture of advocacy and change.

6. A Legacy of Justice and Courage

In this reimagined reality, Emmett Till's name would be synonymous with justice rather than victimhood. His story would serve as a powerful reminder of the importance of accountability and the courage to stand against hate. As society reflects on this legacy, it would inspire ongoing efforts to ensure that no other child falls victim to racial violence or injustice.

The Montgomery Bus Boycott (1955-1956)

The Montgomery Bus Boycott, which took place from December 5, 1955, to December 20, 1956, was a pivotal event in the American Civil Rights Movement. Sparked by the courageous act of Rosa Parks, who refused to give up her seat to a white passenger on a segregated bus, the boycott became a powerful symbol of resistance against racial segregation and injustice.

At the time, Montgomery, Alabama, like many cities in the South, enforced strict racial segregation laws, known as Jim Crow laws. These laws mandated that African Americans sit at the back of public buses and give up their seats to white passengers if the front section was full. Rosa Parks, a 42-year-old African American seamstress and a respected member of her community, had long been active in the struggle for civil rights. On December 1, 1955, after a long day at work, Parks boarded a bus and took a seat in the "colored section." When the bus became crowded, the driver ordered her and three other African American passengers to give up their seats for white passengers. While the others complied, Parks quietly refused, leading to her arrest.

Parks' arrest quickly galvanized the African American community in Montgomery. Led by local civil rights leaders, including a young minister named Martin Luther King Jr., the community organized a mass boycott of the city's bus system. The boycott was intended to last just one day, but its success led to it being extended indefinitely. African Americans, who made up about 75% of the bus system's ridership, refused to use the buses, opting instead to walk, carpool, or find alternative transportation.

The boycott presented significant challenges for the African American community, as many depended on public transportation to get to work, school, and other essential activities. Despite these difficulties, the community remained steadfast, showing remarkable resilience and solidarity. Churches played a crucial role in sustaining the boycott, serving as meeting places for strategizing and organizing carpool systems.

As the boycott gained momentum, it attracted national attention, highlighting the harsh realities of segregation in the South. The leadership of Martin Luther King Jr. became instrumental in guiding the movement, as he emphasized nonviolent resistance and the moral high ground in the struggle for equality. King's powerful oratory and commitment to nonviolence inspired both African Americans and sympathetic whites across the country.

The city's response to the boycott was harsh. White citizens and city officials employed a range of tactics to try to break the resolve of the boycotters. African American leaders were harassed, arrested, and threatened with violence. Some protesters were even physically attacked, and bombings targeted the homes of King and other boycott leaders. Despite these acts of intimidation, the movement continued, driven by a deep sense of purpose and the desire for justice.

The boycott lasted for over a year, and its impact on Montgomery's bus system was profound. Financially strained by the loss of revenue and under increasing pressure, the city's leadership sought to resolve the situation. The legal battle that ensued culminated in a landmark decision. On November 13, 1956, the U.S. Supreme Court ruled in Browder v. Gayle that segregation on public buses was unconstitutional, effectively ending the legal basis for segregation on public transportation.

On December 20, 1956, the Montgomery Bus Boycott officially ended. African Americans returned to the buses, now free to sit wherever they chose. The success of the boycott was a major victory for the Civil Rights Movement, demonstrating the power of collective action and nonviolent protest. It also marked the rise of Martin Luther King Jr. as a national leader in the struggle for civil rights.

The Montgomery Bus Boycott is remembered as a defining moment in the fight against racial segregation in America. It showed that ordinary people, when united by a common cause, could challenge and dismantle deeply entrenched systems of oppression. The boycott not only desegregated Montgomery's buses but also set the stage for future civil rights victories, inspiring generations to continue the fight for justice and equality.

The Assassination of Martin Luther King Jr. (1968)

The assassination of Dr. Martin Luther King Jr. on April 4, 1968, marked one of the most tragic and pivotal moments in American history. As a prominent leader of the Civil Rights Movement, Dr. King had dedicated his life to the struggle for equality, justice, and peace. His death not only shocked the nation but also underscored the deep racial tensions that persisted in the United States, even in the face of progress.

Dr. King was in Memphis, Tennessee, at the time of his assassination to support striking African American sanitation workers who were demanding better working conditions and fair wages. The strike had become a symbol of the broader struggle for economic justice, a cause that Dr. King had increasingly focused on in the final years of his life. On the evening of April 3, 1968, he delivered what would become his final public address, famously known as the "I've Been to the Mountaintop" speech. In this speech, Dr. King reflected on the movement's achievements, the challenges ahead, and his own mortality, eerily suggesting that he might not live to see the ultimate victory of the cause.

The following day, as Dr. King stood on the balcony of the Lorraine Motel in Memphis, he was struck by a single bullet fired from a nearby boarding house. The bullet, fired by James Earl Ray, a known criminal and fugitive, hit Dr. King in the neck, severely wounding him. Despite being rushed to St. Joseph's Hospital, Dr. King was pronounced dead at 7:05 p.m. He was only 39 years old.

The news of Dr. King's assassination spread rapidly, plunging the nation into grief and outrage. His death sparked riots and protests in over 100 cities across the United States, as African Americans expressed their anger and frustration over the loss of a leader who had fought tirelessly for their rights. The violence that erupted in the wake of Dr. King's death reflected the deep-seated racial divisions that persisted in

America, despite the progress that had been made through the Civil Rights Movement.

In Washington, D.C., Baltimore, Chicago, and other major cities, the unrest was particularly intense. Buildings were set on fire, businesses were looted, and clashes between protesters and police were widespread. The government responded by deploying the National Guard to restore order, but the damage had already been done. The riots highlighted the pervasive inequality and racial injustice that still plagued the nation, even as civil rights legislation had begun to dismantle the legal structures of segregation.

Dr. King's assassination also had a profound impact on the Civil Rights Movement itself. While it was a devastating blow to the movement's morale, it also galvanized activists and leaders to continue the fight for equality. In the years following Dr. King's death, his vision of nonviolent resistance and his commitment to social justice continued to inspire new generations of leaders and activists. The movement expanded its focus to include economic justice, anti-poverty initiatives, and opposition to the Vietnam War, causes that Dr. King had passionately advocated for in the last years of his life.

The assassination of Dr. King also led to significant legislative changes. Just days after his death, Congress passed the Civil Rights Act of 1968, also known as the Fair Housing Act, which prohibited discrimination in the sale, rental, and financing of housing based on race, religion, national origin, or gender. This legislation was seen as a tribute to Dr. King's legacy and a recognition of the need to address the systemic inequalities that he had fought against.

Over the years, Dr. King's legacy has been commemorated in various ways. His birthday, January 15, was eventually established as a national holiday, Martin Luther King Jr. Day, celebrated annually on the third Monday of January. Monuments, schools, streets, and buildings have been named in his honor, ensuring that his contributions to the struggle for civil rights are remembered and celebrated by future generations.

The assassination of Martin Luther King Jr. remains a stark reminder of the dangers faced by those who challenge injustice and inequality. It also serves as a testament to the enduring power of Dr. King's message of nonviolence, love, and justice. His death, while a tragic loss, did not mark the end of the struggle for civil rights. Instead, it reinforced the importance of continuing the fight for a more just and equitable society—a fight that Dr. King dedicated his life to, and a fight that must continue in his memory.

Understanding the Cause of Pain

It hurts every time I see the news and learn that another African-American has taken the life of one of their own. It makes me wonder how we can move forward when we're hurting each other. This happens because we still have unresolved anger and a lack of respect for one another, partly due to how society treats us. That's why understanding and compassion are so important.

The Root of the Problem:

The way things are in society often causes us to take out our anger on those closest to us or on someone who looks like us. You've probably heard the saying, "Hurt people hurt people." This is true. Sometimes, when people are frustrated and angry, they lash out at others around them because they can't confront those who are really to blame. This is why we need to turn to God, forgive each other, and try to love and understand one another. If we want equality, we must first give it to each other.

The Danger of Politics Over Humanity:

When someone dies, discussions often become political rather than focusing on the fact that a human life was lost. It's sad that people talk about these deaths from a political standpoint instead of seeing the humanity in the situation. I remember when my cousin passed away, killed by another African-American. As my family and I were dealing with the tragedy, we saw hurtful comments online, blaming Democrats. It angered me because they didn't even know if my cousin was a Democrat or Republican—he was just a person. The problem with society is a detachment from humanity, especially when people who aren't part of our community pass judgment without understanding our struggles.

The Root Causes of Violence in Our Community:

We are lost because we don't know our history and have been manipulated. Who taught us that money is worth killing for? Many of the presidents on our money were slave owners, and now people are killing each other over that same money, which has turned into blood money.

It's ironic that people will kill their own brother or sister for a piece of paper. Have you ever wondered why money is green? Just like fake jewelry that turns your skin green, money has a way of corrupting people. Some people hurt others just to put food on the table or to buy nice things, but that's because they didn't get the financial support they needed to close the generational wealth gap.

Generational Wealth Disparities:

When you have financial backing, you can do things that others can't. In many Black families, if someone needs to borrow money, they might have to ask several family members just to come up with the amount they need. In contrast, a Caucasian family member can often get the money they need from just one relative, and they can likely go back to that same person for help again and again because of generational wealth.

The Strategy Behind Our Struggles:

Crime is often linked to a lack of money. If you don't believe that there was a plan to turn African-Americans into villains by placing them in poor communities with limited resources, then you're wrong. It's heartbreaking to see our Black brothers and sisters struggle, knowing that they could do so much better if given the chance.

The Impact on Our Community:

It's devastating to see another mother cry over the loss of her child because someone in our community decided to take a life over something as worthless as money. There is a lot of anger and hate in our community, and it's causing us to turn on each other. We need to learn to work together.

If we ever receive reparations, we will have to use that opportunity to build a better future for our children and their children. We need to stop hurting each other and start working together.

Education and its Legacy in the Black Community

The roots of educational disenfranchisement in the African American community trace back to the very beginnings of slavery in America. From the outset, slave masters understood the power of education as a tool for liberation and self-empowerment. As a result, they took deliberate measures to prevent their enslaved individuals from learning to read or write. Ignorance was not just a byproduct of their oppression; it was a strategic means to maintain control.

Slave owners feared that an educated enslaved person would become aware of their humanity and potential for resistance. They believed that literacy could spark rebellion and disrupt the status quo. As a result, teaching enslaved people to read was often met with severe punishment. This systematic denial of education was a deliberate act of dehumanization, one that perpetuated the cycle of oppression and limited the possibilities for future generations.

As the shackles of slavery were removed, the legacy of educational deprivation continued to haunt the Black community. The struggle for access to education became a central focus of the civil rights movement, yet the effects of centuries of systemic exclusion lingered. Many African Americans were left grappling with limited resources and inadequate educational opportunities, which contributed to high rates of illiteracy and educational underachievement.

Today, while significant strides have been made toward educational equity, disparities still exist. Many African Americans continue to face challenges in accessing quality education due to factors such as systemic racism, socioeconomic barriers, and underfunded schools in predominantly Black neighborhoods. The generational impact of these disparities creates a cycle where the lack of education and opportunity becomes a curse that is passed down from one generation to the next.

This generational curse is not merely a reflection of individual choices or abilities but rather a manifestation of systemic inequality that has persisted over time. It is a reminder of how historical injustices continue to shape the present, affecting access to education and the overall socio-economic status of the Black community. The cumulative effects of this educational deprivation contribute to cycles of poverty and limited upward mobility, reinforcing the narrative of inferiority that has plagued African Americans for centuries.

of color to claim that African-Americans were uneducated before they came to America. However, this point lacks validity. Understanding a new language, especially when being forced into it, is not an easy task. Africans had their own languages and educational systems before arriving in America. Their comprehension and knowledge would have been understood within their own educational frameworks in Africa.

The institution of slavery stripped them of their native tongues and forced them to adopt a foreign language. The Europeans, fearing the knowledge that Africans might eventually comprehend, deliberately kept them from learning too much. Now, over fifteen decades later, the ripple effects of those actions have caused a stigma on African-Americans. Despite these challenges, African-Americans have climbed the ladder of educational status and acquired the same amount of knowledge as Caucasians.

The difference between Caucasians and African-Americans today lies not in education, but in financial resources. It's important not to confuse this with a lack of education. A more accurate term would be a lack of resources. Generational wealth was not passed down to African-Americans as easily as it was to Caucasian Americans, who often had connections and resources through family members in various professions. These are two different situations, and one should not be confused with the other.

African-Americans are highly educated, both in their own languages and in the European language, English. I have focused on this topic for quite some time, trying to determine how to approach this chapter. Africans have long been treated as the "black sheep" in the American family, and it is unfair to judge a group of people who were killed and slaughtered for learning about themselves and becoming educated. Africans had to pretend they didn't know what they were learning, all while secretly being taught.

The Plan to Separate Black Families

Have you ever wondered why so many Black men were not present in their families' households during the 1980s and 1990s? It wasn't just a coincidence; it was part of a larger plan to separate African-American fathers from their families. This separation weakened the family structure by preventing fathers from instilling principles, life lessons, and guidance from a male perspective.

During these times, government assistance was crucial for many poor families to survive. However, there was a catch: in many neighborhoods, Black men had to stay out of the house for their families to receive this financial help. If a father was found living at home, the family risked losing the assistance they desperately needed. As a result, many Black men felt forced to leave, either voluntarily or involuntarily, which led to a widespread perception of Black fathers as deadbeats.

This system put Black families in a difficult position. Fathers didn't want to be caught at home when inspectors came to check if their families genuinely needed help. Without this assistance, families could barely get by, so many fathers stayed away to ensure their loved ones could survive. However, this arrangement created significant problems in many Black family relationships.

By removing fathers from the home, the system gained control over the mothers and children left behind. With only one parent, who was often busy working, children received less guidance and had more freedom to get into trouble. This situation fed into the stereotype that African-Americans needed someone to oversee them, as if they were incapable of managing on their own.

While it's true that some families split up on their own, the government played a significant role in this separation. By taking fathers out of the home, they stripped away the principles that would normally be taught within a stable household. This was just another way to control the Black community after their history had already been destroyed. Currency—money and resources—became a powerful tool to exert control over African-American families.

Will This Ever Change

I start off this book right after a debate on social media where a guy was being very disrespectful towards African Americans, expressing that they are lazy and have nothing better to do but collect welfare. I got quite upset at just the nerve of hearing someone non-colored express how he felt about African Americans. This is why I believe the school system has failed America. If that guy really knew his history, he would understand that African Americans were never considered lazy. If anything, they were the ones doing most of the work. This is how we have so many historical buildings and how we have so many inventions created by African Americans.

I want to make it known that there are businesses still living off the generational wealth of those who enslaved Africans and profited from their work, wealth that has now been passed down to generations, making their families very wealthy. This is why I feel that reparations should automatically be given with no questions asked. But, of course, I don't believe I'll see this happen in my lifetime, nor in the many generations to come, because we are still living in an America that proudly announces its hate. For instance, there is a building they call the White House. I wonder why they call it that. It holds very important and powerful people for eight years to dictate what's going on in America, even at times forcing their agenda around the world. If that's not a bold statement of control, then I don't know what is.

For a long time, many African Americans have been under the impression that if they don't give up and keep hope, eventually there will be a day when they will get credit and compensation for what they've been promised. Even I believed that at one point. But the more I experience life in America, the more I witness nothing but letdowns. I will say there has been a little progress that we have overcome—or halfway, really, that is the question. Every time I get into these discussions with non-African American citizens, they always try to cover up why society in the Black community is so corrupt, and how, if left to us, we would destroy each other. They even go to the extent of expressing that if it wasn't for us being enslaved, we wouldn't have the language or lifestyle we have in America, as if we benefited so much by being here.

I beg to differ, because if that was accurate, then why are we still fighting for equal rights and equality when it comes to injustice in America? Every time I turn on the news, I see another form of racism being pushed onto people by law enforcement. The corruption even leaks over to the political side of the field. There is so much more I could get into on this topic that your ears would probably bleed. I have family members of all nationalities, from different backgrounds and walks of life, so my point of view is not from any racist perspective, because I love everyone. I just want justice and equal rights for everyone.

The more I research reparations and how other countries around the world have provided reparations for their past mistakes to the next generation, the more I realize that America will just not do right when it comes to African Americans. It's as if Africans will always be considered of less value, no matter what college degree, political view, or quality of life they live. Because of the fact that they are a minority in America, their efforts will always be considered slim compared to the majority.

Unfortunately, I don't think this will ever change when it comes to understanding the blood, sweat, and tears that African Americans have suffered for many years, and still do. There was a time when African Americans were not even considered human. There was a time when African Americans couldn't vote, eat, drink, or use the bathroom in the same facilities as the majority, Caucasians. The unfairness, cruelty, and injustice in society at the time were much more massive than they are currently, I must admit. If it wasn't for those African Americans in that generation fighting for the benefits that we take for granted in its current state, I doubt that things would have ever changed. It took almost 500 years.

I don't think people grasp what a lifetime of misery times five feels like. For experimental purposes, I close my eyes, go into a deep thought process, and imagine waking up in that time when slavery was legal. I'm in a shed, being forced out of bed to go work in the hot, blazing sun, picking cotton and getting whipped by chains for resisting. Just the thought alone makes my skin crawl. It is so easy for someone disconnected from the culture and from having empathy for African Americans to easily sweep murder and human trafficking under the rug, as if it never happened. Or for those who do admit that it happened, they justify it as if the Africans brought to America were the lucky ones. Of course, some of them died here, were hung, and were forced into enslavement, but at least they were in the land of the free. Yeah, but you forgot one thing: we still aren't free yet.

Holding a whole group of people down, taking their resources and finances, putting them in projects, experimenting on them, leaving them there, planting drugs, laughing at the outcome, and then blaming them for how things turned out—these things will never be admitted. For that to be acknowledged, they would also have to admit that reparations should be in effect. And more digging and research would show that not only financially are African Americans owed, but also the businesses that profited off of slavery and were handed down generation to generation. The lands around America would belong to African Americans. For that to happen, it would mean unraveling America from the root, and doing so would, they feel, destroy America. Well, I'm sorry, but it would be the only way to fix the system.

The truth is we have all been lied to about history and the current reality. Everything we work hard for every day to pay bills should be free. This is supposed to be the land of the free, right? Everything that God has given us on this planet, someone has found a way to claim it and sell it. I never understood how land was stolen in America, and to this very day, across America, certain states impose property taxes on land you supposedly bought. Then we can get into the food we eat that God put on the planet for us all to enjoy, but man has found a way to claim and sell it. It seems like nothing has changed; the ways of the past have always been, even now. It seems like it's an algorithm, a pattern of stealing something, claiming it, and selling it. You get the picture.

I used to hear the majority of people getting into these deep conversations about how their tax dollars are paying for a certain group of people, who are minorities in America, being lazy, sitting around collecting checks off of the average worker's income.

Letter to Future Presidents: A Call for Reparations

This is to show you how serious I am about ensuring that future generations, even if I don't get the chance to see it done in my lifetime, witness justice finally being served. I am writing this letter to the future presidents of America, urging them to undo the horrors that were inflicted on this country by granting the descendants of Africans the equal rights that were promised to their ancestors after they were freed from slavery.

The promise of 40 acres and a mule was never fulfilled. I believe that writing a letter to the presidents of the future may help inspire them to correct this historical wrong. Books have been known to outlast lifetimes, and you never know what brilliant leader might read these words and decide to grant the request of the descendants of Africans. It is my hope that this message will help pave the way for justice to be realized for those who have waited far too long.

As an African American, I write to you as a representative of the people, standing united in our call for reparations. This is not merely a demand for financial compensation, but a plea for justice and recognition of the deep-seated wrongs inflicted upon our ancestors and the lasting impacts that continue to shape our lives today.

For over 400 years, African Americans have endured unimaginable suffering—torn from our homeland, shackled in chains, forced into slavery, and subjected to systemic racism that persists to this day. No amount of money can ever truly compensate for the pain, the loss, or the generational trauma that has been passed down. But reparations are a symbolic and necessary step toward addressing the immense debt that this nation owes to its African American citizens.

The promise made to our ancestors, who were promised "40 acres and a mule" as a form of restitution, has yet to be fulfilled. The time has come for the United States to acknowledge its debt and take action to make amends. This is not just a matter of financial reimbursement; it is about fulfilling a moral and constitutional obligation to treat every citizen as equal, to rectify the wrongs of the past, and to create a future where the contradictions of our founding principles are resolved.

Let this be the final chapter in the long and painful history of slavery and its aftermath. Let it be the beginning of a new era, where justice, equality, and true unity are the foundations of our nation. The debt must be paid, and with it, we can move forward together, as one people, towards a future where all are truly free.

Sincerely,

[Darnell L King-Cason]

A Citizen for Justice and Equality

I know that I wrote a letter in this book, dedicated to the president of the future who is willing to start on reparations, but I must add: I pray for you. I know that there will come a time when the mind of a young person wakes up the nation and decides not to follow what the old men have been doing for generations. When this happens, it will change the dynamics of society, but also at the possible cost of their life. Because, let's face it, America doesn't care about explaining their actions. They still haven't cared since all the other acts of controlling the system.

I have examined so many documentaries on the unfortunate leaders being assassinated, and all the lines add up. Enslavement of the mind is now the new slavery in America. Too many think the same way, as if they don't have a mind for themselves. Quite a few have woken up to see the reality we live in, and really, that's all it takes. But I understand now why the leaders who stood for something haven't had a replacement yet—because they would have to know their putting their life on the line for a higher cause. Not everyone is willing to make that sacrifice, which is why society is the way it still is.

But remember, nothing is a coincidence in this society. They are chess pieces being moved across the board, and from what history has shown us, we've been in checkmate for a long time.

Low-Income Living

The history of African Americans in the United States is one marked by resilience in the face of systemic oppression. One of the lesser-discussed yet deeply impactful aspects of this history is how African Americans were pushed into urban centers, often forced to live in low-income housing due to economic and social pressures.

After the Civil War and the subsequent abolition of slavery, African Americans sought new opportunities in the North and other urban areas, hoping to escape the harsh realities of the Jim Crow South. However, upon arrival, they were met with new forms of segregation and discrimination. The promise of better jobs and living conditions was overshadowed by systemic barriers that kept African Americans from accessing the same resources as their white counterparts.

The migration to urban centers was not just a matter of choice; it was a matter of survival. African Americans were often barred from purchasing homes in more affluent neighborhoods due to discriminatory practices like redlining. Banks and real estate agents conspired to keep Black families out of certain areas, restricting them to specific neighborhoods, often the least desirable and most overcrowded. These neighborhoods became the breeding grounds for what would later be known as the projects.

The projects, or public housing developments, were supposed to provide affordable housing for low-income families. However, they quickly became symbols of poverty and despair. The conditions in these developments were often substandard, with poor maintenance, overcrowding, and a lack of basic amenities. These environments, coupled with the lack of economic opportunities, trapped many African American families in a cycle of poverty that spanned generations.

For those who were fortunate enough to have stable jobs, homeownership was still a distant dream. The combination of low wages, high costs of living, and discriminatory lending practices meant that many African American families simply could not afford to buy their own homes. Instead, they were relegated to renting in areas where property values were low, and the quality of life was even lower.

The impact of this forced urbanization and economic marginalization cannot be overstated. Living in these conditions not only affected the physical health of African American families but also took a toll on their mental and emotional well-being. The constant stress of making ends meet, coupled with the fear of violence and crime that often plagued these neighborhoods, created an environment where hope was a rare commodity.

Yet, despite these challenges, the African American community continued to push forward. They built strong, resilient communities within these urban landscapes, creating a sense of identity and belonging that transcended the physical conditions of their surroundings. Churches, community centers, and local businesses became pillars of strength, offering support and resources to those in need.

But the reality remains that many African American families were, and still are, trapped in a system designed to keep them in poverty. The legacy of redlining, discriminatory lending practices, and the concentration of low-income housing in urban areas continues to affect generations. It is a painful reminder of the systemic racism that has shaped so much of American history.

As we reflect on this history, it is important to recognize the resilience and strength of those who have endured and continue to endure these hardships. But it is equally important to acknowledge the systemic changes that are needed to break this cycle. Affordable housing, access to fair lending, and economic opportunities must be prioritized if we are to create a future where all Americans, regardless of race, have the opportunity to thrive.

The Welfare System

The evolution of the welfare system in the United States is a complex narrative that intertwines with the African American experience. Born out of necessity during times of economic hardship, the welfare system was initially established to provide a safety net for the most vulnerable members of society. However, its implementation and effects on African Americans reveal a multifaceted story of both benefit and systemic challenge.

In the early 20th century, as industrialization transformed the American economy, many African Americans migrated from rural areas to urban centers in search of better opportunities. However, the reality was starkly different. The Great Migration, while a hopeful endeavor, often led to disillusionment as Black workers faced discrimination in hiring practices and were frequently relegated to low-paying, unstable jobs. This economic marginalization pushed many families into poverty, creating a dire need for support.

The New Deal programs of the 1930s, instituted by President Franklin D. Roosevelt in response to the Great Depression, marked a significant shift in the government's role in providing economic assistance. While these programs aimed to alleviate suffering and stimulate the economy, they often fell short of addressing the specific needs of African Americans. Discriminatory practices were rampant, as many welfare benefits were administered at the state level, allowing local officials to enforce racially biased policies. Consequently, Black families were often excluded from programs designed to provide unemployment benefits, food assistance, and housing support.

Despite these barriers, welfare programs did offer some crucial support for African Americans during this period of economic despair. For many families, government assistance provided a lifeline, helping them meet basic needs and survive in an environment where job opportunities were scarce. The aid allowed families to access food, healthcare, and housing, which were essential for their survival. For those who had lost their jobs due to economic downturns, welfare benefits helped bridge the gap and prevent total destitution.

In the post-World War II era, the landscape began to shift as the civil rights movement gained momentum. Activists fought for equal rights and opportunities, including access to fair employment and welfare support. While the welfare system continued to be marred by systemic racism, the efforts of civil rights leaders brought attention to the injustices faced by African Americans, advocating for reforms that would benefit all citizens, regardless of race.

However, the narrative surrounding welfare began to change in the late 20th century. The system became increasingly stigmatized, particularly as it was associated with African American poverty. Political discourse framed welfare recipients as dependent and unproductive, ignoring the systemic barriers that created these circumstances. This shift in perception had profound implications for African Americans, many of whom relied on welfare as a crucial support mechanism.

Despite the stigma, it is important to recognize that welfare provided essential resources during times of economic uncertainty. It served as a means of survival for countless African American families who faced barriers to employment and systemic discrimination. The struggle for dignity and equal access to economic opportunities continues, underscoring the need for a more equitable welfare system that acknowledges the historical context of racial inequality.

As we look back on this chapter in American history, it is crucial to understand that welfare was not merely a handout; it was a necessary response to systemic failures in providing equal economic opportunities. The welfare system's legacy is intertwined with the struggles and resilience of African Americans, reflecting the ongoing fight for justice, equality, and the right to thrive in a society that has often marginalized their contributions.

If The Roles Were Reversed

Have you ever considered what it would be like if the roles were reversed? Imagine if, instead of Africans being enslaved for over 400 years, it was the Europeans who endured that fate. Imagine the Europeans struggling to survive, barely managing to make ends meet while being confined to inner-city developments.

Picture this: when it comes to your family history, you have no knowledge beyond the 1800s, if even that far back. The only thing you know is that your ancestors from that era were slaves. Europeans, like your family, helped build the United States, including the Black House, but every time you request a little reimbursement for the part your ancestors played in America's history, you're made to feel as though their pain and suffering didn't amount to anything. The money made off the cotton fields went straight to the black masters, while your ancestors toiled in agony.

Now, every time someone seeks your vote, they make promises—promises that are never kept. As a descendant of enslaved Europeans, how would you feel? Would you simply brush it off, thinking, "At least we were taught something"? Or would you be upset, angry, and tired of asking for something that should have been given long ago?

It's easy to talk about something when you have no personal connection to it, especially when you're in a position of control. But when you place yourself in someone else's shoes and realize that you've been handed the short end of the stick, your perspective changes. You begin to understand the pain and suffering that others went through, and you quickly demand change because the injustice becomes personal.

Consider this analogy: when someone passes away and leaves behind life insurance, the money isn't going to bring that person back. Yet, you owe it to your loved one who paid those premiums every month so that you wouldn't have to struggle after their passing. It's not just about the money; it's about honoring their efforts and sacrifices.

This is the same scenario for enslaved Africans. They paid with their blood, sweat, and tears for 400 years. What they left behind is owed to their descendants. It's not just about reparations—it's about acknowledging their humanity and the legacy they left behind.

Understanding this, how would you feel if you were in their position? Would it be so easy to dismiss the past, or would you stand up and demand what's rightfully yours?

400 years of reimbursement

The best way for us to begin to fix America is to realize it's actually broken. That realization is the only way forward. If we keep justifying why things are the way they are, then nothing actually happens. It gets looked down upon, as if that's just the way things are. African Americans are often told they need to be civilized, but my question is, what were Africans before they came to America? They spoke in their own native tongues. They studied their own cultural beliefs. So, how do you take a group of people who were "nobodies" before you got them and turn them into civilized people? They were "somebody" before you kidnapped them. Once we realize that human trafficking is a crime by itself, and that everything that happened after that was also a crime, it will be the start of understanding why something that happened long ago needs to be fixed.

There's too much blood, tears, pain, and agony that comes with the conversation of paying for what was done, and quite frankly, there's never enough money or land to repay what was done to African descendants—now African Americans. I hear excuses that it was such a long time ago, and that the law allowed for what happened to happen, so now that things have changed, and African Americans are free, let's leave it alone; let's not bring up old things from the past. The only reason why I believe that is being said is because a certain group of people don't want to feel guilty for what happened to Africans—and I really don't care. They don't care for African Americans to be on the same level as them. Financial control is always going to be the reason, because without control of the system, it takes away their power.

It's so easy to talk down on African Americans living in the ghetto, to talk about how they're struggling, as if they came to America on their own, knowing their family history, still being able to speak their native tongue, and having generational wealth to build on to pass down to their offspring—which is totally not true. The reality is, at this point, it shouldn't even be looked at as a handout. Looking at statistical charts shows the generational wealth gap between African Americans and Caucasian Americans. It should be greatly understood, with the background differences in financial wealth, who it was that had a head start in life versus the other.

It is so obvious why reparations need to be given. I'm not talking about doing a petty study from 60 years ago and having the same result at this present time. I'm talking about real progress. African Americans are tired of hearing the same lies over and over in order to get the African American vote. Promises are made but unkept. I recognize it's not going to be cleaned up in one year or even 20 years the way it should be, even with financial reimbursement, because this is not just a 20- to 30-year situation; this accumulated for over 400 years. So, this is going to be our overall 400-year reimbursement. Meaning, just as long as the misery, pain, and suffering of Africans lasted, the descendants of those Africans should benefit for an equal number of years.

This will not only show commitment but also improvement in how the system works in America. It will allow others who are watching to see how America really feels about African Americans, and how that stigma over African Americans of being lazy and not wanting anything in life will disappear. You will see the difference. We have always been creators and inventors of some of the most used technology in the world to this day. When you drive by a traffic light, it should remind you of an African American man. When you look at your cameras to make sure that your house is OK, it should remind you of the inventor, an African American woman.

There's so much that Africans have contributed as Americans. African American history shows that they were never lazy and always creative, very talented. Some of your best sports players, musicians, actors and actresses, teachers, and so on. Everyone who became somebody in life needed to start somewhere, needed a break to get where they are—especially if they were African American. So, we're lucky not every African American is struggling financially, but the facts show that the majority are. I can't forget those who are trying to make it in life, and write them off because a few are financially stable, as if the rest don't matter.

It was never about money. It's about the same thing it is for you and your family. It's about being able to leave something for your family other than rent in the projects, or a mortgage loan that you could barely pay off, or a student loan bill. The truth is, you don't bring people to America, pretend like you have to take care of them, then abuse them and push them into areas by force. Then, years later, once African Americans start realizing that the land they worked hard on and helped build offers them nothing to pass down to their generations, you want to make them feel like it's their problem when they never caused the problem from the beginning. The only way to fix it is to fix it—make right what you made wrong.

Violence in the black Community

The history of violence within any community is a profound concern that demands attention, understanding, and comprehensive solutions. Among the many facets of this issue, the statistics surrounding violence among African Americans reveal a complex narrative, shaped by historical, social, and economic factors. This analysis aims to explore the statistics related to violence in African American communities, examining the underlying causes and the urgent need for a holistic approach to address this critical issue.

Statistical data related to violence in African American communities often highlight a troubling reality. According to the FBI's Uniform Crime Reporting (UCR) Program, African Americans represent a significant percentage of both homicide victims and offenders. For instance, a report from the Centers for Disease Control and Prevention (CDC) indicates that young Black males are disproportionately affected by gun violence, making them one of the highest-risk demographics for both victimization and perpetration.

In 2019, the CDC reported that homicide was the leading cause of death for Black males aged 15 to 34. Additionally, while Black Americans make up approximately 13% of the U.S. population, they accounted for nearly half of all homicide victims during that period. These statistics paint a stark picture of the violence that plagues African American communities, yet they only scratch the surface of a much more complex reality.

To understand these statistics fully, it is essential to consider the historical context of systemic racism and inequality that has long affected African American communities. The legacy of slavery, segregation, and discrimination has resulted in socioeconomic disparities that continue to perpetuate cycles of poverty and violence. Limited access to quality education, healthcare, and economic opportunities contribute to environments where crime can flourish.

Moreover, the War on Drugs and mass incarceration have disproportionately targeted Black communities, further exacerbating the conditions that lead to violence. A report from the Sentencing Project found that Black Americans are incarcerated at more than five times the rate of white Americans, a reflection of systemic biases that not only criminalize poverty but also perpetuate violence as a means of survival in marginalized communities.

Gun violence is a significant factor contributing to the high rates of homicide within African American communities. Studies indicate that gun homicides disproportionately affect Black individuals, with firearms being the leading cause of death in this demographic. According to a 2020 report from the Gun Violence Archive, Black Americans were involved in nearly 60% of all gun homicides, further underscoring the need for a comprehensive approach to addressing gun violence.

Efforts to combat this issue must consider not only the availability of firearms but also the social conditions that lead individuals to resort to violence. Community-based interventions, such as violence interruption programs, have shown promise in reducing gun violence by addressing the root causes and providing support to at-risk individuals.

The statistics surrounding violence in African American communities often contribute to harmful stereotypes and stigmas that perpetuate a cycle of fear and misunderstanding. The narrative that frames Black communities solely as violent overlooks the resilience, strength, and unity present within these neighborhoods. It is crucial to recognize that violence is not inherent to any race or ethnicity; rather, it is a symptom of deeper societal issues.

Media representations frequently exacerbate these stereotypes, focusing disproportionately on crime stories while neglecting the positive contributions of African Americans to society. A more balanced portrayal can help shift public perception and encourage more constructive discussions about violence and its underlying causes.

Addressing the violence in African American communities requires a multifaceted approach that includes community empowerment, systemic change, and investment in resources. Grassroots organizations play a critical role in advocating for policy changes, promoting education, and providing support services to those affected by violence. By fostering community-led solutions, we can begin to break the cycle of violence and promote healing.

Additionally, addressing systemic issues such as poverty, education, and access to healthcare is essential for creating sustainable change. Policy reforms aimed at reducing economic disparities, investing in education, and expanding access to mental health services can help create environments where individuals feel safe and supported.

The statistics surrounding violence in African American communities tell a complex story, shaped by a myriad of historical and contemporary factors. While the numbers may seem overwhelming, they also highlight the urgent need for understanding, compassion, and action. By addressing the root causes of violence and investing in community empowerment, we can work toward a future where all individuals, regardless of their background, can thrive in safe and supportive environments. It is through this collective effort that we can begin to dismantle the cycles of violence and build a more just society for everyone.

Self-Genocide

Exploring the challenges faced by the Black community in America necessitates addressing the harsh truth of self-hatred—a profound internal conflict rooted in a lengthy history of oppression and systemic racism. This self-hatred has fueled cycles of violence and crime, culminating in what resembles self-genocide, with individuals causing harm to themselves and their communities.

From the onset of slavery, African Americans endured dehumanization designed to erode their identity and self-esteem. Enslaved people were conditioned to believe their worth was solely in their labor and were often subjected to brutality to reinforce inferiority. This systematic belittlement cultivated an association of Blackness with frailty, unworthiness, and disgrace. These notions, embedded over generations, perpetuated self-hatred within the community.

As Black individuals absorbed these detrimental perceptions, the repercussions appeared in various ways, including criminal behavior. The exasperation and rage from past and present injustices have led some to engage in self-destructive actions against themselves and their community. In settings where opportunities are scarce and systemic obstacles remain, a diminished sense of self-worth can propel individuals towards harmful conduct, perpetuating cycles of violence and crime.

Self-genocide is a concept that arises when individuals, often unconsciously, partake in the deterioration of their own community through violent and criminal acts. This issue is intensified by socioeconomic conditions such as poverty, educational disparities, and unemployment, fostering a climate of hopelessness. When people feel ensnared in a system with scant prospects for improvement, self-hatred can lead to behaviors that inflict further damage on their community.

Furthermore, the depiction of Black individuals...

Letter to My Black Brothers and Sisters

We really need to get back to loving each other. The news is not a good example to represent us or how we feel about each other. Too many times, I see Black brothers and sisters being killed by the hands of our own. I just pray that God leads you away from the negativity and all of the tricks that have been set up for us from the beginning. Drugs have been placed into our neighborhoods as well as guns because they knew that with us being focused on getting the finances they promised, in many cases, they sent the poison for us to give to our brothers and sisters. Knowing that we need the money and there's no other option due to the petty laws that incarcerate you and turn you into a felon, it's now hard for you to get a reasonable job for your family.

There was no other option but to go out and hustle. They tricked us, made us believe that we achieved something, knowing we would be satisfied as long as we had food on the table to provide for our families. They set us up. We don't have to look over our shoulders for the KKK anymore; they sent us to do it—self-genocide—for the money that they promised us. I bet you if they had given us the 40 acres and a mule a long time ago, there would be no need for us to adapt to the lifestyles that, in some cases, we were forced into. Some people say these are excuses, poor excuses. But I ask you, where are the resources? Every time there is public funding for the kids to do something positive, the politicians are quick to take it away and give the money somewhere else, out of the United States. Yet they call it an excuse to be involved in community activities. That's the only route for a Black man or woman to survive when it's time to pay the bills.

So I say, my Black brothers and sisters, don't fall into the trap. They knew that the music would put us in a trance. They saw in Africa how we used to dance to the drum and how it influenced us, and now look at what it's doing to us—self-genocide. I myself fell victim to listening to rap music. My particular favorite era was in the '80s because it was positive, but when the '90s came, it became negative. I gotta be honest, we can do better. We gotta stop this.

The Importance of Remembering Our Ancestors' Struggles

We've become so accustomed to the life we live in today's society. While it may not be perfect, we've settled into it. However, as I dive deeper into researching slavery, I realize how much we've forgotten the importance of sticking together. We've lost sight of our ancestors' struggles. Yes, we talk about reparations because we see the lingering effects of everything that happened, but as an African who is American, I must admit that we've forgotten the immense challenges our ancestors faced—especially during the Civil Rights Movement of the 1950s and 60s, continuing into the 70s and 80s.

During those decades, it seemed like real change was on the horizon, and we became comfortable. I understand why—on the surface, it appeared that progress was being made. But without financial stability for every African-American who is a descendant of enslaved Africans, there will never be true peace. Sure, people may pretend to love one another, but deep down, this is where self-hatred stems from. We know we deserve better. If we truly remembered everything our ancestors endured, we would appreciate life as we know it much more. There would be no senseless violence among us, no robbing or killing. There would be respect and harmony toward one another. But the only thing that separates us from that ideal is the financial gap.

Why do you think drugs were introduced into our communities? Who do you think put them there to be sold? Why do you think the majority of African-Americans in urban neighborhoods are the ones selling drugs? They're not doing it for their health—it's for the money. Why do you think people resort to robbing, stealing, and killing? It's not because they enjoy it; it's because of the financial desperation.

America has a history of creating its own villains. Africans, in their homeland, were living peacefully, unaware of many of the problems African-Americans are now blamed for. Yet, these victims of human trafficking—our ancestors—couldn't even receive the basic respect and decency of a proper apology or compensation. That's the least that could have been done, considering all the lives that were taken.

We've become too comfortable hurting each other over the so-called "slave master's paper"—money. We're still fighting to be free, regardless of how much wealth we might accumulate, even if we do get reparations. The reason we need to stick together is simple: if you don't respect your own people, how can you expect anyone else to respect you?

Only If We Was All Truly Free

Imagine if America could truly be free—not just in mind, not just in equality, but free. Picture a society where you're no longer forced to pay the electric bill, gas bill, or water bill, or even property tax. Just live your life. It would be a system where people could learn to appreciate each other, enjoy life, praise God, and have no worries. Now, I'm not saying there wouldn't be things to keep us busy, or different ways to occupy ourselves. Everyone would have to play a part in order for this system to work. Instead of working for a check, it would be more like volunteering because everything you do would go towards helping someone else and making society free.

We would have volunteer teachers to teach us what we need to know, volunteer farmers to plant our food, and volunteer chefs to cook it. Doctors who want to pass down their knowledge to future generations would volunteer their services. Nothing would really change—except the title. Instead of "work," it would be called "volunteering." I think that would reset America, making it the land of the truly free. People would have peace of mind and more compassion for one another. And that's the only way you'd be able to live in this America. Those who didn't want to participate could go elsewhere in the world. This wouldn't be a dictatorship; it would be a voluntary movement for those who want to live a better life in the land of the free.

We're a bunch of God-fearing people who serve, praise God, and live the way He intended. I know what you're thinking—this sounds like a fantasy world. And you'd be right because, back to reality, this could never happen. It wouldn't happen because people are too selfish. Instead of working together, they'd rather pull each other down. Society has run its course on America, especially the great minds that think alike but are too afraid of judgment or elimination to voice their brilliant ideas.

Nothing was given to America; everything was taken—from the story of Christopher Columbus to the history of African Americans, all the way down to the middle class and the poor. The more we delve into this book, the more it becomes clear how "divide and conquer" has set the stage for America from the beginning. I want to take a deep dive into the dynamics of how separating one class of people to go against another, with orchestrated music of destruction, has created small-minded people who are unaware of how they're being controlled. And because these small-minded people are the majority in American society, they feel like they're better than the minority.

I am a descendant of my grandparents' grandparents, who were slaves, and I think about how the timeline from when my relatives were enslaved to the present day is really not that long. We're not in control of the year we're born, and I thank God—my Lord and Savior, Jesus Christ—that I wasn't born in that time. I don't think I would've been as strong as my ancestors were.

A Caucasian friend once asked me, "Why do African Americans feel so strongly about the past when it comes to slavery? Why do they treat it as if they were the ones personally enslaved?" I hastily responded, "The reason why we take it as such is because we still see the effects to this day. My people are still in poverty. My people are still struggling, not knowing themselves or where they came from. They can only trace their lineage back a few generations. My people are frustrated, not knowing that this anger was passed down through the bloodline from generation to generation. It was my people who built America, yet we're called lazy every chance someone gets. It's my people who are shoved into communities, with some family members living in the projects for generations. My people are searching for a better day when they can be compensated for the generational wealth gap that was promised but never fulfilled."

This isn't a Handout

Reparations for African Americans are not simply a matter of financial compensation; they are a profound acknowledgment of the deep-seated injustices that have shaped the experiences of millions of people over centuries. The idea of reparations is rooted in the recognition that the United States, as a nation, has a moral and legal responsibility to address the lingering effects of slavery, segregation, and systemic racism. This chapter will explore the historical context, legal foundations, and moral imperatives that support the need for reparations, presenting a comprehensive case for why such measures are not only justified but necessary.

To understand the necessity of reparations, one must first grasp the historical trajectory of African Americans in the United States. The legacy of slavery, which began with the arrival of the first enslaved Africans in Jamestown, Virginia, in 1619, laid the foundation for centuries of exploitation and dehumanization. Enslaved Africans were stripped of their freedom, forced to work in brutal conditions, and denied any semblance of human rights. This system was not only tolerated but codified into law, allowing for the economic exploitation of Black bodies to build the wealth of a nation.

The abolition of slavery in 1865 did not mark the end of racial injustice. Instead, it was followed by the Black Codes, Jim Crow laws, and other forms of legalized discrimination that sought to maintain the social and economic dominance of white Americans. African Americans were denied access to education, employment, and housing, and subjected to violence and terror, all under the watchful eye of a government that failed to protect them. The Civil Rights Movement of the 1960s, while a pivotal moment in American history, only began to scratch the surface of the systemic issues that continue to plague African American communities.

The call for reparations is grounded in the legal principles enshrined in the U.S. Constitution, particularly the Equal Protection and Due Process Clauses. The 14th Amendment's Equal Protection Clause guarantees that no state shall "deny to any person within its jurisdiction the equal protection of the laws." However, the lived reality for African Americans has been a continuous denial of this protection, from the era of slavery through to the present day. Reparations can be viewed as a necessary remedy to address this ongoing violation.

Additionally, the Due Process Clauses of the 5th and 14th Amendments protect against the deprivation of life, liberty, or property without due process of law. The systemic racism that has persisted in the United States represents a violation of these protections, as African Americans have been consistently deprived of their rights and opportunities without adequate legal recourse. Reparations would serve as a form of restitution for these violations, providing a legal mechanism to address the harm inflicted on African Americans over generations.

There are also historical precedents for reparations that support the legitimacy of such claims. The Civil Liberties Act of 1988, which provided reparations to Japanese Americans interned during World War II, is a significant example. This legislation acknowledged the wrongs committed by the U.S. government and provided a form of compensation for the harm caused. Similarly, various treaties and settlements with Native American tribes demonstrate that the U.S. government has recognized its responsibility to make amends for past injustices. These precedents underscore that reparations are not a novel concept but rather a recognized remedy for state-sanctioned harm.

The argument for reparations is further strengthened by the stark evidence of economic and social disparities that exist between African Americans and other racial groups. These disparities are not incidental but are the direct result of historical and systemic discrimination. African Americans, on average, have significantly lower levels of wealth and income compared to their white counterparts. This wealth gap is a direct legacy of slavery, segregation, and discriminatory practices such as redlining, which denied African Americans access to homeownership and wealth-building opportunities.

Social disparities are equally pronounced. African Americans face higher rates of poverty, unemployment, and incarceration, as well as lower levels of educational attainment and life expectancy. These outcomes are not merely the result of individual choices but are deeply rooted in the systemic barriers that have been erected to maintain racial inequality. The psychological impact of this systemic racism is also profound, contributing to generational trauma that continues to affect African American communities today.

Beyond the legal and economic arguments, reparations are also a moral and ethical imperative. At its core, the call for reparations is a call for justice—a demand that the United States acknowledge the wrongs it has committed and take responsibility for the harm it has caused. This is not about assigning blame to individuals but about holding the nation accountable for the policies and practices that have perpetuated racial inequality.

Reparations are also about healing. The wounds of slavery and systemic racism run deep, and they have not yet healed. Addressing these wounds requires more than just words; it requires concrete actions that demonstrate a commitment to justice and reconciliation. Reparations, in this sense, are not just about financial compensation but about restoring the dignity and humanity of those who have been wronged.

There are various ways in which reparations could be implemented, each aimed at addressing the multifaceted nature of the harm done. One approach is direct financial compensation to the descendants of enslaved people, calculated based on the unpaid labor of their ancestors and the economic disadvantage imposed by discriminatory practices.

This compensation would provide a tangible acknowledgment of the harm done and help to bridge the wealth gap that persists today.

Another approach is to invest in African American communities through targeted initiatives in education, healthcare, housing, and economic development. These investments would address the structural inequalities that continue to disadvantage African Americans and provide opportunities for future generations to thrive.

Policy reforms are also a critical component of reparations. Systemic changes in areas such as criminal justice, voting rights, and employment discrimination are necessary to dismantle the barriers that perpetuate racial inequality. By addressing these systemic issues, reparations would not only provide redress for past harms but also lay the foundation for a more just and equitable society.

Please Explain Why Not for African-Americans Reparations

In the complex tapestry of American history, there lies a narrative that demands reflection and accountability—particularly regarding the treatment of immigrants and the descendants of enslaved individuals. As the nation moves forward, it finds itself at a crossroads, where it must confront the disparities in how it supports different communities and why the historical injustices faced by African Americans continue to go largely unaddressed.

America has some explaining to do. The contrast between the financial assistance provided to immigrants and the persistent lack of reparations for African Americans raises critical questions about the nation's values and priorities. For years, the U.S. government has implemented various programs aimed at supporting immigrants, recognizing their contributions to the economy and society. From the Refugee Resettlement Assistance Program, which provides up to $1,125 per month for a limited time, to access to Medicaid and the Supplemental Nutrition Assistance Program (SNAP), immigrants have received substantial financial support as they navigate their new lives.

The Refugee Resettlement Assistance Program alone exemplifies this commitment. Under this program, refugees can receive cash assistance for up to eight months, helping them settle into their communities and establish a foundation for a new beginning. The government has invested heavily in this initiative, reflecting a societal recognition of the importance of supporting those who come seeking refuge and a better life.

Yet, while immigrants are welcomed with a myriad of support systems, the descendants of enslaved individuals—who have faced centuries of systemic racism and economic disenfranchisement—are still waiting for the acknowledgment and compensation they deserve. The historical promise of "forty acres and a mule" made to formerly enslaved individuals after the Civil War remains unfulfilled, and the lack of reparative measures has left African Americans to grapple with the enduring impacts of slavery.

The median wealth of white families, according to the Federal Reserve, is approximately ten times greater than that of Black families, a glaring statistic that highlights the ongoing economic disparities rooted in historical injustices. While America has recognized the plight of various marginalized groups and provided reparations to some—most notably Japanese Americans who were interned during World War II—African Americans have been left without similar redress.

As America has allocated substantial resources to assist immigrants—over $1.6 billion for workforce development programs and emergency housing vouchers—questions arise: Why hasn't the same commitment been made to address the historical injustices faced by African Americans? The legislative efforts to establish reparations, such as H.R. 40, which seeks to create a commission to study reparations, have faced resistance, reflecting a reluctance to confront uncomfortable truths about the nation's past.

America must acknowledge that the disparity in support sends a powerful message: while the contributions of immigrants are recognized and celebrated, the struggles of African Americans remain marginalized. This inconsistency fosters feelings of disenfranchisement among Black communities, who have fought tirelessly for recognition, justice, and equality.

The commitment to welcoming immigrants must not overshadow the obligation to address the historical wrongs faced by African Americans. Reparations are not merely a matter of financial compensation; they are an essential step toward healing the deep wounds inflicted by slavery, Jim Crow laws, and ongoing discrimination. A comprehensive approach to reparations could include direct financial payments, investment in education, and economic opportunities aimed at dismantling systemic barriers.

America stands at a pivotal moment, tasked with the responsibility of reconciling its past with its present. The conversation around reparations and support for immigrants invites a broader reflection on the nation's identity and values. By investing in the well-being of historically marginalized communities, including African Americans, alongside welcoming newcomers, America can strive to create a society that honors its diverse history and builds a more equitable future.

It is time for America to engage in a candid conversation about its priorities, to recognize the interconnections of its immigrant and African American communities, and to take meaningful steps toward addressing the disparities that have persisted for far too long. In doing so, the nation can work towards a future that genuinely reflects its founding principles of liberty and justice for all.

Paying Homage

As I sit and reflect on the freedoms we enjoy today, I am filled with a deep sense of gratitude for the brave souls who paved the way for justice and equality. These individuals, through their courage and determination, challenged the very fabric of a society that sought to deny Black people their rightful place in this world. Their legacy is not just a chapter in our history books—it's a living testament to the power of perseverance and the strength of the human spirit.

I want to take a moment to pay tribute to Dr. Martin Luther King Jr., whose vision of a world where people are judged not by the color of their skin but by the content of their character still echoes through the corridors of time. His leadership and the peaceful yet powerful way he carried his message were instrumental in awakening the conscience of a nation.

We must also remember John F. Kennedy, who, though not perfect, played a crucial role in advancing civil rights legislation. His willingness to stand up and speak out for what was right, even when it wasn't popular, helped push the movement forward at a critical time.

Rosa Parks showed us that one person's courage can be the spark that ignites a movement. By refusing to give up her seat, she reminded us that sometimes the most powerful stand we can take is simply standing our ground.

Malcolm X taught us the importance of self-respect and the need to take pride in who we are. His journey from a troubled past to a leader who fiercely advocated for the dignity and rights of Black people is a story of transformation and empowerment.

The Little Rock Nine, who faced unimaginable hostility just to go to school, remind us of the price of progress. Their bravery in the face of such hatred is a testament to the resilience of the human spirit.

We cannot forget Medgar Evers, who dedicated his life to fighting for civil rights in Mississippi. His tragic death was a stark reminder of the dangers faced by those who dared to demand change, but it also strengthened the resolve of those who continued the fight.

Fannie Lou Hamer, with her powerful voice and unyielding spirit, fought tirelessly for voting rights. Her words and actions remind us that true change often requires us to speak out, even when it's uncomfortable or dangerous.

Bayard Rustin, a brilliant strategist whose work behind the scenes helped to organize some of the movement's most pivotal moments, deserves our recognition. Despite the challenges he faced, including discrimination within the movement itself, he remained steadfast in his commitment to justice.

Thurgood Marshall's victories in the courtroom laid the groundwork for many of the legal protections we now take for granted. His role as the first African American Supreme Court Justice is a powerful symbol of how far we've come, and how much further we still have to go.

Ella Baker believed in the power of ordinary people to create extraordinary change. Her work behind the scenes empowered countless individuals to take action, showing that leadership isn't about being in the spotlight, but about lifting others up.

James Baldwin's writings challenged America to confront its racial issues head-on. His words continue to inspire us to think critically about the world we live in and our place within it.

And to the countless others whose names may not be as widely known but whose contributions were no less significant—freedom riders, activists, organizers, and everyday citizens—I offer my heartfelt thanks. Your sacrifices, your courage, and your determination have made a lasting impact that continues to shape our world.

As I honor these heroes, I also recognize that the work is far from finished. It is now our responsibility to continue the fight for justice and equality, to carry forward the torch that they so bravely lit. The state of the Black community today, with all its triumphs and challenges, is a reflection of their legacy. It's a legacy that we must protect, nurture, and pass on to the next generation.

To the members of the Civil Rights Movement, I say thank you. Thank you for your bravery, your vision, and your unwavering commitment to making the world a better place. Your efforts have given us the freedom to dream, the strength to stand, and the courage to continue the fight for a more just and equitable world.

Final Thoughts

Thank you for taking the time to read my book. I truly appreciate it, and I hope you've learned something new about the history of slavery. I encourage you to delve deeper into this history, as understanding the past is crucial for shaping a better future. The only way to change the future is to act in the present, and the only way to effectively act in the present is to prepare for the future.

Remember, what works for you can also work against you. If a particular perspective benefits you, it's important to recognize that another viewpoint might challenge it. I know that's a bit of a mind twister, but I hope you take away the idea that humans come in all different shapes, sizes, and forms. We must learn to respect each other, regardless of color or background.

The only way to truly fix America is to fix all of America, not just half of it or a small portion. We must come together as a nation and address our challenges collectively—that's the true American way, not the old way.

God bless you and your family. To my brothers and sisters, no matter your color, remember that God loves you. I love you as I love myself, my neighbors, and my friends. Peace be with you.

And by the way, look out for America, You Have Some Explaining to Do: Part Two.